Especially for

....

From

....

Date

....

A BETTER DAY
IS COMING

A BETTER DAY
IS COMING

Encouraging Devotions for Followers of Jesus

GLENN HASCALL

BARBOUR
PUBLISHING

Cover Design: Greg Jackson, Thinkpen Design

Published by Barbour Publishing, Inc., 1810 Barbour Drive, Uhrichsville, Ohio 44683, www.barbourbooks.com

Our mission is to inspire the world with the life-changing message of the Bible.

Member of the
Evangelical Christian
Publishers Association

Printed in China.

INTRODUCTION

Have you ever been frustrated by the unfairness of life? Have you ever seen selfish, dishonest, immoral people get ahead in the world? Or wondered why *you* struggle with health, financial, or relationship issues? Have you ever asked yourself. . .wait for it. . .if being a Christian is really worth it?

That's a tough nut to crack, isn't it? But it's also nothing new. Thousands of years ago, a musician named Asaph wrestled with the same things. "Surely God is good to Israel," he began, in the 73rd Psalm, "to those who are pure in heart."

But. . .

"But as for me," he continued, "my feet had almost slipped; I had nearly lost my foothold." Why? "For I envied the arrogant when I saw the prosperity of the wicked."

Asaph was frustrated by the unfairness of life, having seen the selfish, dishonest, and immoral getting ahead in his world. "They have no struggles," he complained. "Their bodies are healthy and strong. They are free from common human burdens; they are not plagued by human ills. Therefore pride is their necklace; they clothe themselves with violence. From their callous hearts comes iniquity. . . ." He goes on, but you get the picture. And then Asaph asked the big question: Is it really worth it to follow God? "Surely in vain I have kept my heart pure and have washed my hands in innocence."

Whew.

Not surprisingly, as part of God's Word, Psalm 73 comes around to say that, *yes*—it is worth it to follow God. When Asaph "entered the sanctuary of God," he realized that those seemingly trouble-free people he envied faced a disturbing end. But for Asaph, a better day was coming.

"I am always with you," he finally sang to God. "You hold me by my right hand. You guide me with your counsel, and afterward you will take me into glory. . . . My flesh and my heart may fail, but God is the strength of my heart and my portion forever."

That's a message we as Christians need to remember today. No matter how hard your personal circumstances may be, no matter how dark the world grows, *a better day is coming*. It may be in this life, on this earth—God is certainly strong and generous enough to heal your disease, advance your career, restore your marriage, or give you someone to love.

But though He can and sometimes will do these things, for His own mysterious reasons, He also often withholds them. What we can say for sure is that "a better day is coming"—that day we actually live with Him, when the perfection of heaven is our eternal reality, when sin and sickness and sorrow are banished forever from His (and our) presence.

And that's the ultimate message of this book. These 180 devotional readings will encourage you, like Asaph, to take the long view of our short life. Yes, it can be hard. Sure, we wish and pray for blessing. But even when God allows disappointment in your life, know this: *A Better Day Is Coming*.

SCRIPTURES QUOTED: PSALM 73:1, 2–3, 4–7, 13, 17, 23–24, 26

8

UNIVERSALLY TROUBLED

*[Jesus said] "In this world you will have trouble.
But take heart! I have overcome the world."*

JOHN 16:33 NIV

Trouble. You've been introduced, right? You'd be grateful if trouble skipped a visit. That's understandable. You probably do everything you can to avoid it. The trouble with trouble is it's guaranteed. God promised trouble, but He is "our refuge and strength, an ever-present help in trouble."

There isn't one concept in this book that will have any meaning if not for the verse at the start of each reading. They weren't picked out of thin air. They weren't randomly chosen by dropping a finger onto a randomly opened page of the Bible. They were carefully chosen to encourage you, the reader. Most importantly, they are God's words. They speak truth, shed light, and share hope. So don't skip over the opening scriptures—they're the best part of this book. How important was scripture to Jesus? "Heaven and earth will pass away," He said, "but my words will never pass away."

Here's some good news: trouble has never been the final word. It never will be. Jesus overcame every bit of trouble that messes with your day, your emotions, and your decision-making.

Maybe you caused your own trouble or maybe it came from someone else. It doesn't matter. Trouble was never reserved only for people who make bad choices. Trouble is universal. Everyone faces it—but not everyone faces it alone.

SCRIPTURES QUOTED: PSALM 46:1; MATTHEW 24:35

FAITH IS THE VICTORY

For every child of God defeats this evil world,
and we achieve this victory through our faith.

1 JOHN 5:4 NLT

Your life can be defined by victory. But in order to have victory, you must first face opposition. *Victory* is a war word. It applies to the one who wins. Is that you?

You may think you don't live in the vicinity of victory. *Defeated* seems your default setting. The evil around us can be defeated, but only those who are part of God's family can participate in the win. Victory can take place, but only when you trust in God's ability to help. Like the old hymn says, "Faith is the victory that overcomes the world."

The Chinese Christian leader Watchman Nee developed this point well when he said, "Outside of Christ, I am only a sinner; but in Christ, I am saved. Outside of Christ, I am empty; in Christ, I am full. Outside of Christ, I am weak; in Christ, I am strong. Outside of Christ, I cannot; in Christ, I am more than able. Outside of Christ, I have been defeated; in Christ, I am already victorious." How meaningful are the words "in Christ."

You have victory over trouble—in Christ. You share in a victory that *He* wins. You overcome because He overcame. Your trust in the Winner means *you* win. How can you know? "[God] gives us victory over sin and death through our Lord Jesus Christ."

If you want victory, you *will* face trouble. At the end of your life, though, victory remains—because every trouble will finally be over. *Every single one!*

SCRIPTURE QUOTED: 1 CORINTHIANS 15:57

GOD STEPS IN

*[In heaven,] God shall wipe away all tears from their eyes; and
there shall be no more death, neither sorrow, nor crying, neither shall
there be any more pain: for the former things are passed away.*

REVELATION 21:4 KJV

If the best life you'll ever know is right-here-right-now, is it any wonder so many people are unhappy? Your right-now-life doesn't seem to qualify for "best" status.

But trouble keeps you looking forward to God's better day. Don't convince yourself that this temporary home is permanent. Don't think these are the best of times. Don't believe they have to be or trick yourself into thinking they can be. What is this life? "It is even a vapour, that appeareth for a little time, and then vanisheth away." But a better day is coming.

The idea isn't to escape trouble. You can't. Allow God to work *through* trouble, because He will. Some days are smooth. You might enjoy the ride. Other days? Not so much. We get comfortable when life's easy, but there's a purpose behind the unhappy disruptions.

Ever felt like you're living outside your comfort zone, you rarely catch a break, and you just need help? You do need help. If welcomed, God will step in and do His best work to repair what's broken. Those repairs, read-justments, and recalibrations should remind you of a good God whose best day for you will last forever. Remember, Jesus promised He would "prepare a place for you."

What if the best life you will ever live. . .isn't here at all?

SCRIPTURES QUOTED: JAMES 4:14; JOHN 14:2

A BIGGER DREAM

By faith Abraham, when called to go to a place he
would later receive as his inheritance, obeyed and went,
even though he did not know where he was going.
HEBREWS 11:8 NIV

When you have a God-sized dream, don't allow your age, appearance, background, net worth, or race to stand in His way.

God has a dream for you. But you might not recognize it if it doesn't look exactly like your dream.

Abraham had plans, but he reached his golden years without achieving the one thing he had dreamed of for so long—a son. God told Abraham, "Go from your country, your people and your father's household to the land I will show you." And Abraham was "seventy-five years old when he set out."

Abraham probably wouldn't have chosen to wait until he was a hundred years old to have a son. And he might not have chosen to leave his birthplace and family. But he did because he was seeking God's promised "better day."

You'll experience snapshots of "the best day ever" in this life. Just follow God's plan, demonstrating your trust in Him and willingness to do what He asks. Cooperate with His plan and see miracles in the mundane, hope in the ho hum, and possibilities in the plain and unassuming.

SCRIPTURES QUOTED: GENESIS 12:1, 4

DIRECTED STEPS

For I know the thoughts that I think toward you, saith the LORD,
thoughts of peace, and not of evil, to give you an expected end.
JEREMIAH 29:11 KJV

She wasn't the preferred candidate—easily overlooked and better suited to the role of a maid some said.

Such was the frustrating life of Gladys Aylward. Others couldn't see the call of God leading her to China. But their poor opinions couldn't stop Him. Gladys learned, "There are many devices in a man's heart; nevertheless the counsel of the LORD, that shall stand." She was certain God wanted her in China, so she was going there.

Normal channels to the mission field failed, so Gladys worked and saved what she could. Then she heard of a missionary named Jeannie Lawson who needed someone to take over her work in China. In 1932 Mrs. Lawson asked Gladys to come to China, and Gladys spent her life savings to get there.

Gladys thrived in China. She stopped a prison riot, led one hundred orphans out of harm's way, rescued children from slavery, and shared Jesus passionately. She came to be known as *Ai-weh-deh* (Virtuous one).

God used a woman from a working-class family to bring aid to men, women, and children. Though not born in China, she became a citizen. And though she'd struggled to learn the Mandarin language, she eventually spoke it fluently. In the end Gladys was convinced, "A man's heart deviseth his way: but the LORD directeth his steps."

SCRIPTURES QUOTED: PROVERBS 19:21, 16:9

COMFORT'S SOURCE

*God is our merciful Father and the source of all comfort. He comforts us
in all our troubles so that we can comfort others. When they are troubled,
we will be able to give them the same comfort God has given us.*

2 CORINTHIANS 1:3–4 NLT

Reassurance radiates from today's verses. God is the source of *all* comfort.
He's got a corner on the comfort market. And once you've experienced His
soothing presence, He encourages you to share His comfort with others who
live beside you in this society of trouble. Talk about what you've learned and
share the comfort you've been given.

In the 1500s William Tyndale craved comfort. He translated the Bible
in harsh and tedious conditions during dangerous times. In a moment
of complete transparency, Tyndale would say, "My overcoat is worn out;
my shirts also are worn out. And I ask to be allowed to have a lamp in the
evening; it is indeed wearisome sitting alone in the dark."

Life is hard. Some days it emits a foul odor and seems impossible to
face with any kind of grit and determination. Jesus stepped into our world
and understands "our weaknesses, for he faced all of the same testings we
do, yet he did not sin."

Embrace His empathy as you relate to others and "be happy with those
who are happy, and weep with those who weep." This is God's transferable
comfort in troubled times.

SCRIPTURES QUOTED: HEBREWS 4:15; ROMANS 12:15

INSULTED AND BLESSED

Blessed are they which are persecuted for righteousness' sake: for theirs is the kingdom of heaven. Blessed are ye, when men shall revile you, and persecute you, and shall say all manner of evil against you falsely, for my sake.

MATTHEW 5:10–11 KJV

Maybe you've never suffered continual harassment or physical harm for believing in Jesus. But followers of Christ around the world *are* being persecuted right now. Jesus called them blessed because the final answer to ridicule and pain will be forever enjoying God in heaven.

Jesus also said the persecuted would be blessed when criticized, insulted, and slandered because they follow Him.

The persecuted may not be living what others would describe as their best life. But God is clear: "Rejoice, and be exceeding glad: for great is your reward in heaven: for so persecuted they the prophets which were before you."

People may be incensed by the message you share. When Jesus shared the same message for the very first time, people insulted Him. He knows how that feels. You aren't the first person to endure the piercing tongue of a persecutor.

You identify with Jesus when you refuse to respond in anger to persecution. And Jesus taught that "the wrath of man worketh not the righteousness of God." You serve a God who has seen many who've regretted insulting our rescuer, lover of our souls, and forgiver of both the persecuted and the persecutors.

SCRIPTURES QUOTED: MATTHEW 5:12; JAMES 1:20

UNLIKELY RESCUE CANDIDATE

Saul began to destroy the church. Going from house to house,
he dragged off both men and women and put them in prison.

ACTS 8:3 NIV

Paul had a shadowed past—before he was known as Paul the Apostle, he was Saul the Persecutor. He wasn't a prime candidate for rescue because he didn't believe Jesus was the Rescuer.

Saul was a destroyer. At a Christian's fatal stoning, "the witnesses laid their coats at the feet of a young man named Saul." This was the same guy involved in house raids and imprisoning Christians.

If you were a Christian in Paul's vicinity, you couldn't live your best life. He was on a seek-and-destroy mission. He thought he spoke for God, but he thought wrong. . .and people suffered.

You can't be assured of your best life here because many people have no interest in following God, and they might think you stand in the way of their ambitions. They may even demand that you agree with their opinions.

But Saul was transformed. Both his heart and his name were changed when he met Jesus on the Damascus road. Jesus said of Paul, "This man is my chosen instrument to proclaim my name to the Gentiles and their kings and to the people of Israel."

The persecutor became the persecuted. The unbeliever believed. The zealous refocused his passion. Paul's better day dawned at the sundown of this life when he said, "I have fought the good fight, I have finished the race, I have kept the faith."

SCRIPTURES QUOTED: ACTS 7:58, 9:15; 2 TIMOTHY 4:7

NEW MAN MINCAYE

He that covereth his sins shall not prosper:
but whoso confesseth and forsaketh them shall have mercy.

PROVERBS 28:13 KJV

How would you feel if your children called your father's killer "Grandpa"? No, this isn't an emotionally dysfunctional soap opera. It's a true story about how forgiveness changed everything.

Steve Saint was just a boy in the 1950s when his father, Nate, and a few other missionaries spotted the Huaorani tribe on the banks of an Ecuadorian river from their plane. The missionaries landed because they believed that this solitary tribe was interested in knowing more about Jesus. But the tribe killed every missionary, including Steve's dad.

The man who killed Nate Saint was known as Mincaye. For two years, Steve grieved the loss of his father. And Mincaye wondered about the message the missionaries were never given a chance to share.

When Mincaye eventually heard the message, he became a Christian, and Steve miraculously forgave the man who killed his father. Steve and Mincaye became friends, and Mincaye took on the role of grandfather to Steve's children. God had once again raised new life from the ashes of death: "If any man be in Christ, he is a new creature: old things are passed away; behold, all things are become new."

Mincaye couldn't change on his own. He had to "put off. . .the old man" and "put on the new man." When he did, he discovered a reason to believe in the promise of God's better day—the same thing Nate Saint believed.

SCRIPTURES QUOTED: 2 CORINTHIANS 5:17; EPHESIANS 4:22, 24

WHERE SIN CANNOT EXIST

For everyone has sinned; we all fall short
of God's glorious standard.
ROMANS 3:23 NLT

You have broken God's law just as He said you would. You've sinned like every human being. From the very first disobedience until this moment, everyone has failed to be completely faithful to God. No one has ever met God's standard of perfection—except Jesus. Don't try to rationalize things or minimize failure: "If we claim we have no sin, we are only fooling ourselves and not living in the truth."

Your best life can't coexist with sin—yours or someone else's.

Your better day will come only when you live in a place where sin cannot exist. In heaven there is no pain due to the betrayal of broken promises, no need for regret. Faithfulness will be your new choice.

Heaven will be a new experience. There's a reason this will be known as your better day. "No eye has seen, no ear has heard, and no mind has imagined what God has prepared for those who love him." It will be better than you imagine, more stunning than the most brilliant sunrise, and it will be an infinitely better life than you've ever experienced here.

Jonathan Edwards summed up this better day by saying, "To go to heaven, fully to enjoy God, is infinitely better than the most pleasant accommodations here."

Don't seek something that can't be found here. Rejoice in each God moment, and accept those moments as samples of the best that's yet to come.

SCRIPTURES QUOTED: 1 JOHN 1:8; 1 CORINTHIANS 2:9

IF ONLY

A sound heart is the life of the flesh:
but envy the rottenness of the bones.

PROVERBS 14:30 KJV

You are immersed in an "if only" kind of world. If only you had more money, more fame, more stuff. The words *if only* are the petri dish of discontent. Toss in equal parts envy, spite, and covetousness, and watch a sin culture grow out of control. Envy is certain that someone else has something it deserves and demands a balanced scale.

Envying other people is a pretty meaningless pursuit. What is God's remedy? "Let not thine heart envy sinners: but be thou in the fear of the LORD all the day long." Does it make sense to envy people who don't fear God? What they have won't last forever—it's not transferable to the better day coming. And their life is not meant for you. Envy is a wasted energy that could be spent honoring the God who promised something more—something you could never buy, earn, or create on your own.

You can't love well when you envy. It's hard to love someone with jealousy in your heart: "Charity suffereth long, and is kind; charity envieth not; charity vaunteth not itself, is not puffed up." Love makes you look good. Envy distorts the beauty God made for you.

Honor the Author of your better day. He has written your best life.

SCRIPTURES QUOTED: PROVERBS 23:17; 1 CORINTHIANS 13:4

*Eli answered, "Go in peace, and may the God of
Israel grant you what you have asked of him."*

1 SAMUEL 1:17 NIV

God answered Hannah's desperate prayer for a son. The bad news is she'd longed for this child for years while her husband's second wife seemed to have no problem bearing children.

That was tough.

But Hannah knew where to turn—to the very Lord who "had closed her womb." Her oblivious husband said, "Don't I mean more to you than ten sons?"; her rival wife "provoked her till she wept and would not eat"; and the careless priest Eli accused her of drunkenness when she passionately prayed. But those prayers, with bitter tears, moved God's heart to give Hannah a child.

And not just any child—her boy, Samuel, would become a mighty prophet and leader, one who would call God's people back to faithfulness and anoint their greatest king, David.

Would this have happened apart from Hannah's faithfulness in the daily grind of her earlier life? Would this have happened apart from her exhausting, tear-drenched prayers? Would this have happened if she didn't believe that her day was coming?

God wants faithful people who say like Job, "Though he slay me, yet will I hope in him." So stay the course. Stick to your guns. Ask, seek, and knock. God may just give you the desire of your heart.

SCRIPTURES QUOTED: 1 SAMUEL 1:5, 8, 7; JOB 13:15

SUSTAINED AND UNMOVED

Cast thy burden upon the LORD,
and he shall sustain thee: he shall never
suffer the righteous to be moved.
PSALM 55:22 KJV

George Müller lived in 1800s England, and he chose an unusual way to engage in ministry. He told no one of his specific needs—except God. George prayed, God moved, and people helped. George knew that prayer changes things. He once said, "The reason why the children of God are so frequently overpowered by difficulties and trials is because they attempt to carry their burden themselves, instead of casting it upon God, as He not only graciously allows them to do, but commands them to."

George agreed with the psalmist who said, "Blessed be the Lord, who daily loadeth us with benefits, even the God of our salvation."

George founded orphanages that were home to more than ten thousand orphans and created schools that taught more than a hundred thousand students in England. When orphans needed food, George prayed and God answered. When they needed milk, he prayed—and a milk wagon broke down in front of their orphanage.

Jesus said, "My yoke is easy, and my burden is light." George found it was no burden to believe God would meet his needs. His was a life of dependence on a good God. George said, "Though the trial still lasts, the burden. . .is gone, because we have laid it upon God, to bear it for us; but if we have not exercised faith in God, we are still carrying the burden ourselves."

SCRIPTURES QUOTED: PSALM 68:19; MATTHEW 11:30

REVOLUTIONARY THINKING

We destroy every proud obstacle that keeps people from knowing God.
We capture their rebellious thoughts and teach them to obey Christ.
2 CORINTHIANS 10:5 NLT

This book is revolutionary or even radical in a Christian culture that believes followers of Jesus can and should have it all now—that their best life is just waiting for them to embrace it. Every verse in this book is biblical. If these thoughts are revolutionary today then they were equally life-changing before the original ink was dry.

God upsets the status quo: "My thoughts are nothing like your thoughts . . .my ways are far beyond anything you could imagine." Do something radical by allowing God to transform your thoughts to be like His. Begin by reading His Word.

When you're introduced to a new idea, take the time to see what the Bible has to say about it. Don't assume every idea is God's. Take the thought captive. If this were an interrogation then ask questions. Dig deep. There's only one opinion that counts, and it's the opinion of the author of life's instructions. People can't follow God when they believe a lie. You can't follow God with rebellion in your heart.

What the Bible says isn't just something to consider: "Don't just listen to God's word. You must do what it says. Otherwise, you are only fooling yourselves."

Be revolutionary. Be radical. Be honest. Be inquisitive. Be a thought wrangler. Accept what is truth. Learn from the Truth Teller.

SCRIPTURES QUOTED: ISAIAH 55:8; JAMES 1:22

A PRAYER APPROVED

Finally, brothers and sisters, whatever is true, whatever is noble,
whatever is right, whatever is pure, whatever is lovely,
whatever is admirable—if anything is excellent or
praiseworthy—think about such things.

PHILIPPIANS 4:8 NIV

The Bible doesn't say much about Jabez, but his short dialogue with God is important. What we know for sure is that Jabez was more honorable than his brothers, and God answered this prayer: "Oh, that you would bless me and enlarge my territory! Let your hand be with me, and keep me from harm so that I will be free from pain."

Jabez had to believe God was worth following, that He spoke truthfully, had a pure character, and was admirable, excellent, and praiseworthy. By thinking about those things, he became closer to God. The short prayer of Jabez was a prayer God could easily say yes to. Why? Because Jabez wanted more if *God* was the One blessing. Jabez wanted his influence to grow if God guided him and to be able to share God's wonder with people who thought Jabez himself was a nobody.

Your prayers too can receive a yes response from God: "If we ask anything *according to his will*, he hears us. And if we know that he hears us—whatever we ask—we know that we have what we asked of him." This isn't a blank check. God will say yes when your passion fits His plan.

SCRIPTURES QUOTED: 1 CHRONICLES 4:10; 1 JOHN 5:14–15

AN URGING

*Come boldly unto the throne of grace, that we may obtain mercy,
and find grace to help in time of need.*

HEBREWS 4:16 KJV

In the 1890s Annie Clayton and her sister Vanie were sent to purchase wood shavings from a cooper shop in San Jose. This wasn't their first trip, so their mother didn't worry about the young girls.

But Vanie hadn't been feeling well and didn't tell anyone. The girl thought it would pass. On a silent street, with basket in hand, Vanie slipped to the ground. She couldn't take another step. The girls had been taught to pray, so they asked for God's help. They believed He would, and He did.

Before the girls could voice an "amen," a man inside a nearby warehouse felt God's urging to go outside. He wasn't especially thrilled to leave his work nor was he anxious to investigate the urging. The girls saw the man and hoped he would help, but he didn't see them and returned to his desk. The urging came again and again. On the third trip outside his building, he finally saw the girls and with compassion brought them home.

Two young girls and a businessman learned the value of prayer. Didn't God tell Jeremiah, "Call unto me, and I will answer thee"? Didn't Paul say, "Continue in prayer, and watch in the same with thanksgiving"?

Two girls prayed for help, and God turned sickness into a reminder that He is more than faithful.

SCRIPTURES QUOTED: JEREMIAH 33:3; COLOSSIANS 4:2

ASK. SEEK. KNOCK. REPEAT.

"And so I tell you, keep on asking, and you will receive what you ask for.
Keep on seeking, and you will find. Keep on knocking,
and the door will be opened to you."

LUKE 11:9 NLT

You might believe this verse means that God has to give you what you want if you keep asking. Or you might remember that the Bible says, "You can pray for anything, and if you believe that you've received it, it will be yours."

But if this is the complete picture of how God answers prayer, then either God is a liar or there's more to the story—because no one gets everything they ask for. You might come to believe that God lets you down more often than He answers prayer. You might think He says you can have whatever you want but then doesn't deliver on His promise.

But God can't lie, so there must be more to prayer: "When you ask, you don't get it because your motives are all wrong—you want only what will give you pleasure."

The reason you're told to ask and keep asking, seek and keep seeking, knock and keep knocking is not to get your way, but to be assured that the God who always answers prayer gets the final word. . .while you have plenty of time to discover if the request is self-serving or honors God. It's an invitation to spend more time learning what God wants to say yes to.

SCRIPTURES QUOTED: MARK 11:24; JAMES 4:3

BOAST IN GOD'S "NO"

[Paul said] in order to keep me from becoming conceited, I was given a thorn in my flesh. . . . Three times I pleaded with the Lord to take it away from me.

2 CORINTHIANS 12:7–8 NIV

Paul had been a conceited Pharisee who thought he was doing God a favor by persecuting Christians. He may have thought he was God's favorite, but that was before he met Jesus.

Jesus knew the Pharisees were proud of their accomplishments. They enjoyed comparing themselves to the mass of inferior faithful. Pharisees had every reason to believe God would say yes to their requests. They were certain they followed the law better than anyone, and they were experts at boasting. Such was Paul's religious background, but following Jesus was different.

Whatever Paul's thorn in the flesh might have been, he knew it was something that would prevent him from thinking he was better than other people. He must have been comforted when God said, "My grace is sufficient for you, for my power is made perfect in weakness."

Three times Paul asked God to take this "thorn" away, and each time God said no. Paul learned God's plan was better: "That is why, for Christ's sake, I delight in weaknesses, in insults, in hardships, in persecutions, in difficulties. For when I am weak, then I am strong."

When God doesn't say yes to your prayer requests, rejoice. God's no might just be saving you from your own worst self.

SCRIPTURES QUOTED: 2 CORINTHIANS 12:9, 10

REDIRECTED

Trust in the LORD with all thine heart; and lean not unto thine own understanding. In all thy ways acknowledge him, and he shall direct thy paths.

PROVERBS 3:5–6 KJV

Your current setback might just be God redirecting your steps, your epic failure could be God rearranging your priorities to connect with His plan, or what looks like a stop sign might be a delay that leads you to seek direction.

In the 1700s, David Brainerd had a life that was filled with setbacks, failures, and stop signs. His prayer was for fruitful ministry, and yet he was kicked out of college, denied the opportunity to preach, and stricken by tuberculosis. David saw a clear path forward, but God said no.

Instead God planned for David to preach to Native Americans. God's *no* caused David to advise others to "faithfully perform the business you have to do in the world, from a regard to the commands of God; and not from an ambitious desire of being esteemed better than others."

The road to your best life might include setbacks, failures, and stop signs. God may allow you to tread dark roads while saying, "Thy word is a lamp unto my feet, and a light unto my path." Keep reading His Word and you'll receive clarity.

The psalmist knew that God would show him "the path of life." Sometimes God says no to the path you want to take as He did to David Brainerd. Like David Brainerd, trust God's wisdom and good plan for your eternal future.

SCRIPTURES QUOTED: PSALM 119:105; PSALM 16:11

IN SEARCH OF A
SPIRITUAL SIDESHOW

Jesus asked, "Will you never believe in me unless
you see miraculous signs and wonders?"

JOHN 4:48 NLT

Have you ever seen something fantastic at a magic show? Even if what you see is intellectually impossible, you still enjoy the trick.

People often see Jesus as a spiritual sideshow. They want Him to do something miraculous, but as soon as they witness what they can't explain, the wonder diminishes and they dismiss it as a trick. They say they want to believe in God, yet when God shows up, they try to prove He didn't. It's tough to live your best life when you refuse to recognize the Life-giver.

People with this mind-set never say, "I will call on God, and the LORD will rescue me." Instead they call on the Lord but refuse to recognize Him. They mock God and assume He won't notice. They see something they've never seen before but refuse to change how they think about God.

When you share Jesus with someone like this, you are not responsible for their unbelief. You are responsible only for telling what you know.

Signs and wonders confirm God's goodness to those who believe but don't really have meaning for those seeking a good show. And if you're ever tempted to follow in the footsteps of the unbelieving, "Be careful how you live. Don't live like fools, but like those who are wise."

SCRIPTURES QUOTED: PSALM 55:16; EPHESIANS 5:15

SEEK, BEYOND THE MIRACLE

*Even after Jesus had performed so many signs in their presence,
they still would not believe in him.*

JOHN 12:37 NIV

Jesus healed both publicly and privately. He performed miracles witnessed by few and many. The people found Jesus intriguing but weren't convinced enough to follow Him. "Yet at the same time many even among the leaders believed in him. But because of the Pharisees they would not openly acknowledge their faith for fear they would be put out of the synagogue; for they loved human praise more than praise from God."

People can witness the miraculous and suffer from a hard heart, closed mind, and demanding spirit. They expect divine help while forfeiting joy and gratitude.

Maybe miracles seem rare because if they were common, they'd be less appreciated. The people who witnessed Jesus' miracles prove that.

Jesus asks you to trust Him without asking, "What have you done for me lately?" God loves you generously. Can you return His love without making demands? "Without faith it is impossible to please God, because anyone who comes to him must believe that he exists and that he rewards those who earnestly seek him."

Your reward is a better day coming. It's the expectation that God is getting things ready and the certainty that you'll never need to be separated from God's love.

God isn't a genie who grants wishes, a vending machine that dispenses spiritual lollipops, or online shopping with free delivery. He offers miracles of His choosing, timing, and purpose. Recognize it. Welcome it. Appreciate it.

SCRIPTURES QUOTED: JOHN 12:42–43; HEBREWS 11:6

SEEING MIRACLES DAILY

Thou art the God that doest wonders:
thou hast declared thy strength among the people.
PSALM 77:14 KJV

Her family followed Jesus, and she believed He was a big God—a good God. So how could God not reach into His big bag of miracles and deliver one for her? She believed. She prayed. She begged. Yet Joni Eareckson was paralyzed below her shoulders following a diving accident. She knew God could fix this, but He didn't answer in the way she wanted.

God performs miracles every day. Oceans have water. The world has air. New babies experience life. "He is before all things, and by him all things consist."

When Jesus lived among us He healed some people—but not all. Joni suffered but knew that "the God of all grace, who hath called us unto his eternal glory by Christ Jesus, after that ye have suffered a while, [will] make you perfect, stablish, strengthen, settle you."

Joni was denied the miracle of good health. Instead she received empathy for the suffering and eyes that recognize overlooked miracles. For more than fifty years, Joni has helped those who suffer physically. Would she have done so without a life redirection? Like Paul, Joni discovered that God's strength is perfect when, humanly speaking, she's at her weakest.

When God sends His comfort, the best miracle may be the blessing of *recognizing* you've been blessed. Joni knows the promise of her better day, "Whatever troubles are weighing you down are not chains. They are featherweight when compared to the glory yet to come."

SCRIPTURES QUOTED: COLOSSIANS 1:17; 1 PETER 5:10

THE STRUGGLE

The temptations in your life are no different from what others experience.
And God is faithful. He will not allow the temptation to be more than
you can stand. When you are tempted, he will show you
a way out so that you can endure.

1 CORINTHIANS 10:13 NLT

Temptations lead to a struggle that ends in victory or defeat. Your choices are important, and God can help you make the right ones.

If you think that you are facing more difficult challenges than others, Jesus understands because He too battled temptation. God is not treating others with greater preference. He loves you and allows your struggles to fulfill His good plans. He knows you can endure with His help. We fail only when we try to handle life on our own.

Whether it's a trial or a temptation, God can lead you through. Will you trust Him?

"In his kindness God called you to share in his eternal glory by means of Christ Jesus. So after you have suffered a little while, he will restore, support, and strengthen you, and he will place you on a firm foundation."

There is light at the end of the tunnel. Your obedience in the middle of temptation will lead to restoration after your trial. In fact, "don't be surprised at the fiery trials you are going through, as if something strange were happening to you." You're not alone in the struggle. You never have been. God is there in your midst. All you have to do is accept His help.

SCRIPTURES QUOTED: 1 PETER 5:10; 1 PETER 4:12

TEMPTATION IN THE WILDERNESS

Jesus was led by the Spirit into the wilderness to be tempted by the devil.
MATTHEW 4:1 NIV

Jesus didn't give up the role of being God's Son, but He did become human. He experienced pain, suffering, and temptation. He felt both hunger and thirst, and He experienced emotions.

Satan told Jesus, "If you are the Son of God, tell these stones to become bread." Jesus had fasted for forty days and He was hungry, so Satan reminded Jesus that He had the power to turn ordinary rocks into food. If He did, Jesus would not be trusting God's perfect timing.

Satan then took Jesus to the highest point on the temple and said, "If you are the Son of God throw yourself down." Satan knew that God would send angels to help Jesus. If Jesus made this choice, it would suggest that He felt God was far off, unwilling to help.

Finally Satan took Jesus to the top of a mountain and said, "All this I will give you if you will bow down and worship me." Jesus was the perfect sacrifice for sin. To accept Satan's offer would have short-circuited God's plan because sin would be part of His DNA.

Jesus ended the conversation with the perfect reply: "Worship the Lord your God, and serve him only." Jesus' temptation led to a struggle that ended in victory. His victory enables you to refuse Satan's offers too.

SCRIPTURES QUOTED: MATTHEW 4:3, 6, 9, 10

ESCAPE PLAN

The Lord knoweth how to deliver the godly out of temptations.
2 PETER 2:9 KJV

God doesn't sit in heaven wringing His hands, wondering how He can help you when things go south. He doesn't worry that you'll get into trouble. He knows you will. He waits only for an invitation to your crisis.

Temptation affects everyone. You can know the right thing to do and still face a crisis of conscience by justifying wrong choices. Billy Sunday said, "Temptation is the devil looking through the keyhole. Yielding is opening the door and inviting him in."

Billy was a professional baseball player in the late 1800s. Although things were different in baseball at the time, he faced the same old temptations—fame, money, and excess. Scripture predicted this problem: "But they that will be rich fall into temptation and a snare, and into many foolish and hurtful lusts, which drown men in destruction."

Sometimes Billy was unsuccessful in avoiding sin. It was a hymn played at Pacific Garden Mission in Chicago that brought Billy to surrender his plan by submitting to God's. The Lord helped him face temptation and set him on a different path. God promises, "I will instruct thee and teach thee in the way which thou shalt go: I will guide thee with mine eye."

Billy's better day would come, but in the meantime, he had the best walking partner—One who understands temptation and has an escape plan.

SCRIPTURES QUOTED: 1 TIMOTHY 6:9; PSALM 32:8

ACCUSED UNJUSTLY

*O God, whom I praise, don't stand silent and aloof while
the wicked slander me and tell lies about me.*

PSALM 109:1—2 NLT

You've been there, done that, and have the emotional scars to prove it. Someone spread vicious lies about you, and you can't understand why. Unfortunately, friends and family can be just as guilty of spreading hurtful gossip as bullies. And you've probably passed on a rumor or two as well.

But scripture says, "Don't repay evil for evil. Don't retaliate with insults when people insult you. Instead, pay them back with a blessing. That is what God has called you to do, and he will grant you his blessing."

The engine of society runs on revenge, but God offers an alternative fuel that results in a blessing from God rather than a curse from the offended. God wants you to "do good to those who hate you."

It's easy to shift into defensive mode when insults are being hurled your direction. Most people wouldn't blame you. They might even cheer for your rebuttal, but God won't be impressed.

He asks you to pray for people who lie about you, because they need Him as much as you do. They'll answer to God, and so will you. Because of the overwhelming mercy God has shown you, you must also be merciful. You might even turn an enemy into a friend.

Every perfect day is interrupted by life, and bad news never arrives at a good time. Insults transform a good day into one that frays your emotions. But God pours mercy on your difficult times and promises a better day to come.

SCRIPTURES QUOTED: 1 PETER 3:9; LUKE 6:27

WHY ME, LORD?

When his brothers saw that their father loved him more than any of them,
they hated him and could not speak a kind word to him.

GENESIS 37:4 NIV

Joseph lived through unfair treatment. His brothers hated him and sold him as a slave. An Egyptian official's wife wrongfully accused him of sexual assault, and he was tossed into prison. Those he helped forgot about him.

Each time something bad happened, God brought new opportunity to Joseph. When in prison, "The warden paid no attention to anything under Joseph's care, because the LORD was with Joseph and gave him success in whatever he did."

Joseph learned to handle both failure and success. He rose from slave to second in command of a mighty nation. God's plan was not dependent on the accusations of storytellers. Joseph had a God-directed purpose to save millions from a famine. He would later tell his brothers, "You intended to harm me, but God intended it for good to accomplish what is now being done, the saving of many lives."

This young man had to endure the pain of betrayal and loss to discover mercy and restoration.

When you feel that giving up is the only sane option, remember Joseph. He was treated unfairly and lost his family, reputation, and freedom. And when his brothers wondered, "What if Joseph holds a grudge against us and pays us back for all the wrongs we did to him?" Joseph "reassured them and spoke kindly to them."

Trust, beloved, that God has a plan to redeem your pain as well.

SCRIPTURES QUOTED: GENESIS 39:23; 50:20, 15, 21

AT THE END OF SUFFERING

Watchman Nee had dedicated his life to following Jesus. He taught his fellow Chinese about Jesus and started churches.

But the political climate was changing in China. In 1952, Watchman Nee was arrested. He was accused of cheating, bribery, and tax evasion, but his family and friends were certain he was arrested for sharing the Gospel.

Watchman Nee wasn't bitter at being falsely accused and imprisoned. He said, "To remove warfare from a spiritual life is to render it unspiritual. Life in the spirit is a suffering way, filled with watching and laboring, burdened by weariness and trial, punctuated by heartbreak and conflict." Perhaps he remembered that Jesus said, "If they have persecuted me, they will also persecute you."

Watchman Nee agreed with the apostle Peter: "The trial of your faith, being much more precious than of gold that perisheth, though it be tried with fire, might be found unto praise and honour and glory at the appearing of Jesus Christ."

In 1972, Watchman Nee died in prison. When family came to bury the body, they were given a note he had written and placed underneath his pillow: "Christ is the Son of God who died for the redemption of sinners and resurrected after three days. This is the greatest truth in the universe. I die because of my belief in Christ."

Watchman Nee endured the suffering way. You can expect suffering in this world, but rest in the hope of a better day ahead.

SCRIPTURES QUOTED: JOHN 15:20; 1 PETER 1:7

THE ENDURANCE CHAIN

We can rejoice, too, when we run into problems and trials, for we know that they help us develop endurance. And endurance develops strength of character, and character strengthens our confident hope of salvation. And this hope will not lead to disappointment. For we know how dearly God loves us, because he has given us the Holy Spirit to fill our hearts with his love.

ROMANS 5:3—5 NLT

Today you'll connect the links between the problems you face and the joy you'd like to experience.

Everyone has problems to endure. Endurance is the first link in reaching the joy that God promises. Given enough time, you either endure or give up, but when you endure, you shape the next link—good character. And don't forget the link known as hope. This is the expectation that even though you don't always understand why you face problems, you're certain God can take endurance and character and deliver rescue. Rescue completes the link to God's love, and this chain is the perfect length to stretch between your worst day and God's best news.

Scripture says, "Patient endurance is what you need now, so that you will continue to do God's will. Then you will receive all that he has promised." People don't usually want to endure problems, but James said that others notice those who do: "We give great honor to those who endure under suffering."

SCRIPTURES QUOTED: HEBREWS 10:36; JAMES 5:11

WEARY AND WAILING

"I am the only one left, and now they are trying to kill me."
1 KINGS 19:14 NIV

Weariness assaulted the prophet Elijah and nearly won. He lived through three and a half years without rain in difficult circumstances. But God had proven to the evil King Ahab that there was no god but Him, and Elijah had ended the lives of the false prophets of Baal. This should have been Elijah's victory moment.

But Elijah received a death threat from the queen and fear overcame him: "May the gods deal with me, be it ever so severely, if by this time tomorrow I do not make your life like that of one of them," the queen said. And Elijah "was afraid and ran for his life."

Did God's power weaken because of a wicked queen's threat? Not at all, but weariness has a way of exaggerating tragic circumstances. Elijah was very vocal: "I have had enough, LORD."

But God was gentle with His frazzled prophet and sent an angel to deliver food and rest to Elijah. Decisions shouldn't be made when you're exhausted.

Once Elijah was rested, God came to him and said, "What are you doing here, Elijah?" The prophet went back to work.

You might need a break in order to face your problems. Get alone with God. Take some time off if you can, and allow God to speak into your stillness. When the time is right, get back to the work God has for you.

SCRIPTURES QUOTED: 1 KINGS 19:2, 3, 4, 9

A VERY HARD ROAD

Fear thou not; for I am with thee: be not dismayed; for I am thy God:
I will strengthen thee; yea, I will help thee; yea, I will uphold
thee with the right hand of my righteousness.

ISAIAH 41:10 KJV

During World War II, Germany invaded the Netherlands and began arresting Jewish citizens. The ten Boom family hid Jews in their home to keep them safe.

In the winter of 1944, soldiers arrived, arresting more than thirty people, including Corrie ten Boom and members of her family. Within ten days Corrie's dad, Caspar, died. Months later, her sister Betsie also died in a German concentration camp.

Corrie was released in December, but nothing would ever be the same. She was free, but the world she had known a year earlier no longer existed.

Corrie endured great trials and honed strong character by hoping in Christ and His rescue. God used her as a vessel to pour out His love on others. This Romans 5 principal sustained Corrie from her worst experience to a lifelong ministry of reconciliation between those who hurt others and those who've been hurt. She wrestled with personal forgiveness but triumphed. She said, "There is no pit so deep, that God's love is not deeper still." She learned to love as God had loved her.

Hers was a hard road, yet Corrie understood "that all things work together for good to them that love God, to them who are the called according to his purpose." Corrie could easily say, "When I try, I fail. When I trust, He succeeds."

If she could give advice to you today she might utter the words of the psalmist: "Commit thy way unto the LORD; trust also in him."

SCRIPTURES QUOTED: ROMANS 8:28; PSALM 37:5

SACRED EMPLOYMENT

*Work willingly at whatever you do, as though you were working for the
Lord rather than for people. Remember that the Lord will give you an
inheritance as your reward, and that the Master you are serving is Christ.*

COLOSSIANS 3:23–24 NLT

Who is your boss? Does he or she add positivity to your work experience or
drive you to look for another job?

Work environments aren't perfect, but they shouldn't be avoided either.
"Make it your goal to live a quiet life, minding your own business and working
with your hands." Work isn't the problem, and your boss isn't the enemy.
Your willingness to be a good employee has nothing to do with who's wearing
the supervisory title. *God* is your boss. Work for Him and your work ethic
improves, your job satisfaction increases, and the quality of your work is
noticeable. "Commit your actions to the LORD, and your plans will succeed."

Martin Luther described the process this way: "What you do in your
house is worth as much as if you did it up in heaven for our Lord God. We
should accustom ourselves to think of our position and work as sacred and
well-pleasing to God, not on account of the position and work, but on account of the word and faith from which the obedience and the work flow."

On a future better day, you'll get to meet your boss. Wouldn't it be nice
to hear Him say, "Well done"?

SCRIPTURES QUOTED: 1 THESSALONIANS 4:11; PROVERBS 16:3

A JOB FOR A QUEEN

"For if you remain silent at this time, relief and deliverance for the Jews will arise from another place, but you and your father's family will perish. And who knows but that you have come to your royal position for such a time as this?"

ESTHER 4:14 NIV

It wasn't the best of times for Queen Esther. Soon her family would be killed because the king had been tricked into enacting an unjust law.

The king didn't realize he'd signed a death warrant for his queen and her people. But once His seal authorized the law, there was no going back.

Esther had a job only she could do, but it came with a huge risk. If she went to the king without an invitation, she could receive the death sentence. So she instructed her relative Mordecai: "Do not eat or drink for three days, night or day. I and my attendants will fast as you do. When this is done, I will go to the king, even though it is against the law. And if I perish, I perish."

After fasting and prayer, Esther went to the king. He welcomed her and wanted to know how he could help. In time, Esther told her husband how he had been manipulated by his jealous advisor, and the king wrote a new law that balanced the scales: "The king's edict granted the Jews in every city the right to assemble and protect themselves."

The queen's best work started with prayer.

SCRIPTURES QUOTED: ESTHER 4:16, 8:11

THE WORK MOVEMENT

And whatsoever ye do in word or deed, do all in the name of
the Lord Jesus, giving thanks to God and the Father by him.
COLOSSIANS 3:17 KJV

Robert's passion for moving dirt changed the way roads were built and how buildings were constructed. Robert was a jack-of-all-trades, and he'd learned from each of the many jobs he'd held. This hunger for learning contributed to his passion for earth-moving machines, but Robert said, "You will never know what you can accomplish until you say a great big yes to the Lord."

Robert dedicated his life and work to God. Governments were eager to buy his latest inventions, and Robert gave 90 percent of his earnings back to God. He was asked to speak worldwide and again gave 90 percent back to God. Robert believed that he should "be content with such things as ye have: for he hath said, I will never leave thee, nor forsake thee."

Friends called him "God's businessman." Robert worked hard, gave generously, and shared what he knew as he trained others practically. You see, God gave him a work to do, and R.G. LeTourneau decided that because God had done so much for him, he could happily respond as the Bible commands: "Do all to the glory of God."

For Robert, work wasn't a means to get what he wanted but to share what God gave.

SCRIPTURES QUOTED: HEBREWS 13:5; 1 CORINTHIANS 10:31

BANK ON IT

*Whatever is good and perfect is a gift coming down to us from
God our Father, who created all the lights in the heavens.
He never changes or casts a shifting shadow.*

JAMES 1:17 NLT

What would life be like if God proved unreliable? What if there was no way to know whether the sun would rise in the morning or what season was coming next? What if you could never be sure if God would forgive you?

Your assurance of the better day that's coming hinges on your belief that God fulfills promises. Don't wait until the end of your life to decide whether God is faithful and true. And don't believe ideas that cast doubt on God's character.

Walk with Him, and He will prove His unfailing faithfulness to you in countless ways. If you believe God is unfaithful, then you might question if He really loves *everyone*, if His rescue plan has a black list, or if there really is such a thing as a better day coming.

God will keep His promises even if you don't believe He will. But make no mistake, He wants you to believe: "Trust in the LORD with all your heart; do not depend on your own understanding."

Our human understanding is faulty, but God's dependability is a divine promise. We make mistakes. God doesn't. We break promises. But God *keeps* promises. "For all of God's promises have been fulfilled in Christ with a resounding 'Yes!'"

If you long for your better day, start by depending on the God who keeps His promises.

SCRIPTURES QUOTED: PROVERBS 3:5–6; 2 CORINTHIANS 1:20

DANIEL AND GOD
THE DEPENDABLE

"Anyone who prays to any god or human being during the next thirty days, except to you, Your Majesty, shall be thrown into the lions' den."
DANIEL 6:7 NIV

Daniel was a wise man who had the king's ear. Jealous fellow leaders tried to trap him, but Daniel had a habit of doing the right thing. Frustrated, Daniel's enemies decided to exploit his prayer life by having the king decree that those found praying to anyone but the king would be thrown to the lions. But Daniel continued to pray to the only true God three times a day.

The new law went into effect, and the mob of jealous leaders gathered "as a group and found Daniel praying and asking God for help." Now they were certain Daniel's position would be theirs.

The king unwillingly condemned Daniel to the lions' den with these words: "May your God, whom you serve continually, rescue you!" The king waited hopefully for Daniel's God to act.

And God the Dependable showed up. His angels kept the lions' mouths closed, and Daniel was rescued. Because God proved once again His faithfulness, a haughty king came to honor the author of dependability. The king said, "[God] rescues and he saves; he performs signs and wonders in the heavens and on the earth. He has rescued Daniel from the power of the lions."

SCRIPTURES QUOTED: DANIEL 6:11, 16, 27

TEACH MEN TO BE FAITHFUL

The things that thou hast heard of me among many witnesses, the same commit thou to faithful men, who shall be able to teach others also.

2 TIMOTHY 2:2 KJV

If God could transform Dawson (Daws) Trotman, a "liar, gambler, and pool shark," then He can be trusted to renew other lives too.

Daws chose to follow the One he considered trustworthy, and he wanted others to follow as well. If Daws couldn't find faithful followers, then he would teach them to be. A familiar psalm says, "Thy word is a lamp unto my feet, and a light unto my path." Daws knew that, "If you can't see very far ahead, go ahead as far as you can see."

Daws told others how God rescues mankind. He walked with new Christians as they learned and grew and began the discipling ministry known as the Navigators.

When a man who'd learned about Jesus came to Daws and asked him to teach a friend, he refused. He said, "You teach him." God will always help new disciples to become teachers.

Daws held his tattered and marked Bible and agreed with words he'd read many times: "This book of the law shall not depart out of thy mouth; but thou shalt meditate therein day and night, that thou mayest observe to do according to all that is written therein." A faithful God had dependable words for dependent disciples.

SCRIPTURES QUOTED: PSALM 119:105; JOSHUA 1:8

UNCOMMON. ABUNDANT. RICH.

"The thief's purpose is to steal and kill and destroy.
My purpose is to give them a rich and satisfying life."
JOHN 10:10 NLT

Never mistake a materially rich and satisfying life with living God's best life for you today. The two are distinctly different.

God's rich and satisfying life starts with accepting what He's given you. His riches may not be money. His satisfying may not arrive with a new house. Paul made this clear when he said, "I have learned how to be content with whatever I have. I know how to live on almost nothing or with everything. I have learned the secret of living in every situation, whether it is with a full stomach or empty, with plenty or little."

Satan will attempt to steal your hope, kill your dreams, and destroy your trust. God never does that. You may not live in perfect circumstances, but you follow a God who can help you change your perspective, remind you of what He's given, and proclaim that you have something better to look forward to.

Jesus said: "Life is not measured by how much you own." No comparison shopping, keeping up with the Joneses, or pouting when you don't get what you want.

Remember, God gives good gifts, and they're rarely something as common as money. Mathew Henry wrote, "The joy of the Lord will arm us against the assaults of our spiritual enemies and put our mouths out of taste for those pleasures with which the tempter baits his hooks."

SCRIPTURES QUOTED: PHILIPPIANS 4:11–12; LUKE 12:15

INVITATION ACCEPTED

Mary said, "My soul glorifies the Lord and my spirit rejoices in God my Savior, for he has been mindful of the humble state of his servant. From now on all generations will call me blessed, for the Mighty One has done great things for me—holy is his name."

LUKE 1:46–49 NIV

An angel had just delivered to an unwed teenage girl the news that she would have a baby who would be God's Son. But who would believe she had seen an angel? Who would show grace, knowing she was pregnant and unmarried? How could Mary be a spokesperson for abundant living?

But Mary trusted God: "May your word to me be fulfilled." Can it be that simple? It can when you believe God keeps His promises. Her belief sustained her through the neighbors' disapproving whispers, family shame at her growing form, and daily troubles.

Mary's joy came from knowing God was using her as part of His rescue mission for mankind. She witnessed firsthand Jesus' birth, death, and resurrection. How much more abundant does a life need to be?

God asked Mary to accompany Him on a journey. She didn't know the route, she didn't understand the final destination, and she'd be misunderstood. But God invited and Mary "treasured up all these things and pondered them in her heart."

God is also inviting you to a journey—one that carries the promise of an abundant life. Will you take His hand?

SCRIPTURES QUOTED: LUKE 1:38, 2:19

ABUNDANCE DISCOVERED

Christ also suffered for us, leaving us an example,
that ye should follow his steps.

1 PETER 2:21 KJV

Fatherless by the age of four, he worked for room and board as a child because his mother struggled to care for nine children alone. He worked for his uncle as a shoe salesman, which might have been the main reason he remained employed. Most people thought he would have a less than abundant life.

D. L. Moody is a widely recognized name, but at eighteen, no one expected that he'd amount to much. He started a Sunday school class yet struggled to read to the children. He was denied church membership because no one thought he was serious enough.

But Moody disappointed the naysayers by believing God instead of the voices surrounding him. "We are told to let our light shine, and if it does, we won't need to tell anybody it does. Lighthouses don't fire cannons to call attention to their shining—they just shine." In the glimmer of God's goodness, abundance arrived. D. L. knew that the abundance didn't come from himself: "O LORD, I know that the way of man is not in himself: it is not in man that walketh to direct his steps."

A college, publishing company, and church bear the name of this former shoe salesman. Countless lives were influenced by his life of abundance. "Seek ye first the kingdom of God, and his righteousness; and all these things shall be added unto you." Seek God. Discover more abundance than you've ever dreamed.

SCRIPTURES QUOTED: JEREMIAH 10:23; MATTHEW 6:33

HIS STRENGTH

Be strong in the Lord and in his mighty power.
EPHESIANS 6:10 NLT

If you try to be strong apart from the might and power of God, you'll be left with only muscles and brute force. God's strength doesn't make you brutal, it makes you humble. His might does more than impress, but it's impressive. His power changes hearts and minds and prefers mercy to justice.

You have an invitation. Accept it. God's strength can be your strength. His might and power can be yours. When your need matches His plans, He shows up. He never sends you to the front line without the tools you need. He never sends you anywhere expecting failure, so don't leave home without Him.

He sends you with the full backing of the greatest power this world has ever known. "God is our refuge and strength, always ready to help in times of trouble." That's the power you have when you're called, prepared, and sent.

God *will* send you, or maybe He already has. Where you go may be difficult and how you respond will be important. Turn to God's Word for help: "When evil people come to devour me, when my enemies and foes attack me, they will stumble and fall. Though a mighty army surrounds me, my heart will not be afraid. Even if I am attacked, I will remain confident." With God, you can be confident in your victory.

God doesn't ask you to do what you can't. He asks you to do because *He* can. Stand strong in that power. Hang on to His might and tell everybody, "God did that. What a great surprise."

SCRIPTURES QUOTED: PSALM 46:1, 27:2—3

GOD'S STRENGTH SONG

"The LORD is my strength and my defense; he has become my salvation.
He is my God, and I will praise him, my father's God, and I will exalt him."

EXODUS 15:2 NIV

Moses led a choir of over a million. In this case, they really were singing to the choir, and the people needed a reminder of God's faithfulness in this wilderness concert. God freed the people from slavery in Egypt, He delivered them from soldiers who pursued them, and He rescued them from starvation.

God defended the nation of Israel and gave strength to their leader, Moses. He took rebellious people and promised them a home. He offered His strength for their weakness, His hope for their hopelessness, and His future for their past.

No day in the wilderness was a best-life day. People complained, they chased after other gods, and they didn't like what was on the menu. "If only we had meat to eat!" No wonder they needed a reminder song.

They sang, but did they listen to the words their lips were forming? Salvation came from the God of their fathers. He was their defender. He was almighty God.

It's easy to label the Israelites as ungrateful, but God didn't promise room service and resort living on the way to His better day. When you're feeling less than thankful for your current circumstances, remember this: "Who among the gods is like you, LORD? Who is like you—majestic in holiness, awesome in glory, working wonders?"

Discover strength in a wonder-working God.

SCRIPTURES QUOTED: NUMBERS 11:4; EXODUS 15:11

SEEK HIS STRENGTH

My soul melteth for heaviness: strengthen thou
me according unto thy word.
PSALM 119:28 KJV

Susanna Wesley needed strength—a lot of it. She was the mother of nineteen children—nine died in infancy. Her husband would leave for up to a year at a time when he got mad. She once wrote to her husband, Samuel, "I am a woman, but I am also the mistress of a large family. And though the superior charge of the souls contained in it lies upon you, yet in your long absence I cannot but look upon every soul you leave under my charge as a talent committed to me under a trust."

God's strength upheld Susanna, and she stood for God in that strength. Twice her husband was jailed because he couldn't pay bills, and Susanna was left to care for her children without her husband's income. Yet two of her sons would grow to write hymns, preach sermons, and impact nations. John and Charles Wesley did so because they learned the source of strength and witnessed Him in their mother's life.

Susanna obeyed God's Word: "Seek the LORD and his strength, seek his face continually." She could proclaim, "The LORD is my strength and my shield; my heart trusted in him, and I am helped: therefore my heart greatly rejoiceth." With God's strength, the impossible became possible.

Susanna Wesley was "content to fill a little space if God be glorified." She did so by seeking God's strength.

SCRIPTURES QUOTED: 1 CHRONICLES 16:11; PSALM 28:7

ARMOR INTRODUCTIONS

Put on all of God's armor so that you will be able to
stand firm against all strategies of the devil.
EPHESIANS 6:11 NLT

God offers His help to all who stand against the devil's three objectives: distract, defeat, and destroy. The enemy takes his chosen profession seriously: "He prowls around like a roaring lion, looking for someone to devour." So, "stay alert."

God hasn't left you defenseless. He's given you armor that protects and defends your heart and mind against devious strategies designed to make you question the God who gave you life. And He also gave you directions for living.

We're defeated when we question God's directions and seek an alternative. But God's armor is designed to protect you from doubting that He has the best in mind for you and that His ways are superior.

When you agree to follow Him and wear His armor to stand against the devil, you can say, "I will study your commandments and reflect on your ways. I will delight in your decrees and not forget your word."

Each piece of armor has an important purpose, so don't face the enemy without it.

Author John Bunyan knew the perfect first step to donning God's armor: "You can do more than pray after you have prayed, but you cannot do more than pray until you have prayed. Pray often, for prayer is a shield to the soul, a sacrifice to God, and a scourge to Satan."

SCRIPTURES QUOTED: 1 PETER 5:8; PSALM 119:15–16

FOUND FAITHFUL

In the land of Uz there lived a man whose name was Job.
This man was blameless and upright; he feared God and shunned evil.
JOB 1:1 NIV

It's easy to fall for the enemy's traps if you're unprepared for his suggestion that you deserve to have whatever you want. Satan often uses this tactic to lead people away from following God.

Job's faithfulness caught Satan's notice, and the Lord said to Satan, "Have you considered my servant Job? There is no one on earth like him." Satan agreed but didn't like it. The book of Job is the story of a man who lost nearly everything because Satan wanted to watch him walk away from God.

Job is a testament to the truth that when a person trusts God, Satan cannot win. Satan could take things away from Job, but only Job could abandon his faith. The good news is that "Job did not sin by charging God with wrongdoing." He had questions, to be sure, and Job couldn't claim this was his best life. But his faithfulness was rewarded.

Job's experience proved that absolute trust in God brings His protection—and that protection will always be stronger than whatever the adversary dreams up. Satan saw a man shielded by God's armor before the idea was even written in scripture. Maybe this worst-case scenario is recorded to show us that no matter how difficult things get, our trust in God towers above all the experiences we'll ever face.

SCRIPTURES QUOTED: JOB 1:8, 22

NO SON OF SATAN

A new heart also will I give you, and a new spirit will I put within you:
and I will take away the stony heart out of your flesh,
and I will give you an heart of flesh.

EZEKIEL 36:26 KJV

Born in Puerto Rico to a self-proclaimed witch and a satanic priest, Nicky Cruz was described as a son of Satan. In 1953, after Nicky attempted suicide, his father sent him to live with his brother in New York.

Things didn't improve, and he ran away to join a violent gang. If he was a son of Satan, he was acting the part masterfully.

When Nicky met street evangelist David Wilkerson, the preacher said all the right things—but Nicky threatened to kill him. When a psychiatrist proclaimed that Nicky was on his way to hell, the young man believed it. Another time when Nicky threatened David's life, the preacher said, "You can kill me and cut me into a thousand pieces and throw them right there on the street. But every piece will cry that Jesus loves you, Nicky!"

Shock ran through Nicky. Could it be true that Jesus loved him? A son of Satan?

This evangelist needed the armor of God to help a young man who needed a new heart: "For with the heart man believeth unto righteousness; and with the mouth confession is made unto salvation."

Nicky got his new heart and a new position: as a child of God.

Jesus loves you just as much as He loved Nicky Cruz.

SCRIPTURE QUOTED: ROMANS 10:10

A STEAMROLLED SPIRIT

*For we are not fighting against flesh-and-blood enemies, but against evil
rulers and authorities of the unseen world, against mighty powers in
this dark world, and against evil spirits in the heavenly places.*

EPHESIANS 6:12 NLT

Your best life isn't possible when you have an adversary working overtime
to destroy it. If you think you're living it, you may be blind to the problems
you face—or you've settled for an inferior definition of *best*.

You have victory as a child of God, but that victory may not be today. This
world is engaged in a raging spiritual war.

Satan is relentless. He'll attack anytime—day or night. He's quite satisfied
to ruin your good day with his bad news. He doesn't care how hard you've been
trying, and tears don't faze him. He'll steamroll your spirit every chance he
gets. But he's also a liar who "disguises himself as an angel of light." He may
not show up as something evil and frightening. If he can get you to lower your
guard, then he's that much closer to winning the spiritual battle you face.

Let this reality seep into your soul— with offers of a comfortable life, the
enemy will try to draw you away from the place God told you to stand firm.
When you think you can have whatever you want, the thought becomes the
fuel of jealousy and selfishness. This is "not God's kind of wisdom. Such
things are earthly, unspiritual, and demonic."

Follow God and know for certain that your promised future will never
describe today. Keep standing firm. Let God improve your life.

SCRIPTURES QUOTED: 2 CORINTHIANS 11:14—15; JAMES 3:15

DID GOD REALLY SAY?

Now the serpent was more crafty than any of the wild animals the
Lord God had made. He said to the woman, "Did God really say,
'You must not eat from any tree in the garden'?"

GENESIS 3:1 NIV

Adam and Eve were living their best life in paradise on earth, but under one condition. God told the first couple, "You must not eat from the tree of the knowledge of good and evil."

One single rule. They had access to everything else, but they doubted God's goodness and desired the only thing God said was off-limits.

The serpent spoke this doubt-inducing question to Eve: "Did God really say?" Of course God said it. Hadn't He? Doubt crept into Eve's mind. The serpent said, "God knows that when you eat from it your eyes will be opened, and you will be like God."

Didn't God create the world, the sky and sea, the animals and plants? He did. And she could be like Him? She ate the fruit, offered it to Adam, and he too ate. In that moment, they both knew right from wrong. The couple felt regret and shame, but God already had a rescue plan in place for mankind—Jesus.

The chain of sin linked every generation to the sin of a couple who wondered if God really meant what He said. Every generation would need to wait for God's better answer to come.

SCRIPTURES QUOTED: GENESIS 2:17, 3:5

PLANS SURRENDERED

[Jesus] said unto him, Come out of the man, thou unclean spirit.
MARK 5:8 KJV

In her preteen years, farm girl Joanne Shetler thought of a home in the country and cows roaming the hills, not of reaching the demon possessed in remote areas of the Philippines. But God's plans required Joanne to undergo a heart change.

God used a traveling missionary to redirect Joanne's future. That encounter led her to Bible school, training camps, and the mission field. In the 1960s, Joanne became a respected Bible translator. Before she ever got to her destination, Joanne prayed for the people who needed to hear God's Word. Joanne's best-life dreams were altered, amended, and then abandoned. God had better plans.

The people were interested in God. Satan hated this because he'd built a stronghold in the Philippines. Those who were afflicted by evil spirits begged for help. Satan opposed her, but Joanne prayed and God answered. The people began turning to God.

Jesus cast demons out of a man and then said, "Go home to thy friends, and tell them how great things the Lord hath done for thee." Joanne also sent those who'd been rescued home to tell others what God had done, and a spiritual revolution began among the Balangao people.

God's rescue is the best thing that can happen in life. It's a promise that a better day is coming. Satan hates God's rescue plan and he hates losing. But ultimately he will because God wins.

SCRIPTURES QUOTED: MARK 5:19

EVERY SINGLE PIECE

Put on every piece of God's armor so you will be able to resist the enemy in the time of evil. Then after the battle you will still be standing firm.

EPHESIANS 6:13 NLT

Players don't run onto the gridiron half-dressed, and you shouldn't face the enemy that way either. To be fully equipped to resist Satan, we must don every piece of spiritual armor plating available to us.

It's also important to know you're not alone in this battle. Christians throughout the world experience struggles and suffering, but our faith believes God can take bad circumstances and work them into something with a good ending: "Stand firm against him, and be strong in your faith. Remember that your family of believers all over the world is going through the same kind of suffering you are."

God has given you everything you need for spiritual protection. But warriors do get wounded (see the word *suffering* in the preceding paragraph), and we need the care of the Great Physician. God is good, holy, and merciful, and He encourages us: "Be on guard. Stand firm in the faith. Be courageous. Be strong." And He doesn't leave us stranded, because He promises never to leave. Period.

The battles we face aren't unique, unexpected, or even the final word. Someday victory will be final, hope will be rewarded with a promise kept, and the enemy will be crushed. So stand firm today!

SCRIPTURES QUOTED: 1 PETER 5:9; 1 CORINTHIANS 16:13

THE REBUILDING OPPOSED

Tobiah the Ammonite. . .said, "What they are building—
even a fox climbing up on it would break down their wall of stones!"
NEHEMIAH 4:3 NIV

Nehemiah was an Israelite living in exile. He hadn't been home in a long time, but he'd heard sad stories of how Jerusalem was a place of rubble not worship. The people were demoralized not encouraged. And the walls were broken, leaving the people without protection.

Miraculously, Nehemiah's passion for rebuilding the city walls connected with the king, and he sent Nehemiah to Jerusalem. The king even funded the rebuilding project. But Nehemiah faced opposition.

Foreigners had come to Jerusalem, and they didn't want the people to think that Jerusalem would ever be anything more than a pile of stones. While the people were struck with fear, Nehemiah prayed, "Hear us, our God, for we are despised. Turn their insults back on their own heads."

Through God's power, the people repaired the wall in fifty-two days, and they could envision a time when Jerusalem would be filled with worshipers. Enemies had come from every direction, but God sent them home disappointed.

The people needed God's help and protection to do the impossible, and Nehemiah prayed the right kind of prayer: "Now strengthen my hands." He knew that God could do what he could not. He trusted that with God all things are possible.

SCRIPTURES QUOTED: NEHEMIAH 4:4, 6:9

COMMITTED

*The everlasting God, the L*ORD*, the Creator of the ends of the earth,*
fainteth not, neither is weary? . . . He giveth power to the faint;
and to them that have no might he increaseth strength.

ISAIAH 40:28—29 KJV

John Paton was a missionary in the South Pacific who relied on God's armor. The people John served were cannibals who sought to appease their own gods.

Spiritual warfare permeated the environment, but the God who doesn't grow weary helped John to say, "This is strength; this is peace; to feel, in entering on every day, that all its duties and trials have been committed to the Lord Jesus—that, come what may, He will use us for His own glory and our real good!"

The native population tried to kill John many times, but John felt that even this had a positive effect: "I had my nearest and most intimate glimpses of the presence of my Lord in those dread moments when musket, club or spear was being levelled at my life."

Just when he thought the natives would kill him, one chief, and then another, stepped up and dramatically promised to protect the missionaries. John must have thought of Jesus' suffering: "Consider him that endured such contradiction of sinners against himself, lest ye be wearied and faint in your minds." Perhaps that's what led him to proclaim, "Nothing so clears the vision and lifts up the life, as a decision to move forward in what you know to be entirely the will of the Lord."

SCRIPTURE QUOTED: HEBREWS 12:3

WEAR THE BELT

*Stand your ground, putting on the belt of truth
and the body armor of God's righteousness.*
EPHESIANS 6:14 NLT

Why is truth so important? People think you're judgy if you even come close to telling someone they're wrong. Even the whole notion of truth can get a little blurry. The world says truth is relative and we can decide our own truth. But God's Word says that isn't how it works.

Here's the truth about truth: "All Scripture is inspired by God and is useful to teach us what is *true* and to make us realize what is wrong in our lives. It corrects us when we are wrong and teaches us to do what is right. God uses it to prepare and equip his people to do every good work."

Absolute truth removes all the guesswork. It stops you from constantly changing your opinion and helps you recognize the wrong decisions of others. But there's a catch: "We will speak the truth in love, growing in every way more and more like Christ, who is the head of his body, the church."

Truth and love belong together. Truth without love leads to judgmental attitudes. Love without truth leaves people struggling in the same failed decision-making.

God's truth allows you to stand your ground with the confidence that there is a discernible standard. Truth is the belt that holds everything else together.

SCRIPTURES QUOTED: 2 TIMOTHY 3:16–17; EPHESIANS 4:15

TRUTH SPEAKER

Then Nathan said to David, "You are the man!"
2 SAMUEL 12:7 NIV

David was a beloved king of Israel, but perfection wasn't a skill set included on his résumé. He'd sinned, and word had gotten out.

The prophet Nathan arrived in full storyteller mode to address the king's grave error: "There were two men in a certain town, one rich and the other poor." His story captured David's attention as he had been both rich and poor.

The poor man's family had a pet lamb. A rich farmer with countless sheep lived nearby. Yet when a guest arrived at the rich man's home, he didn't want to decrease his flock, so he went to the poor man's house and stole his pet lamb to feed to his guest.

When David heard the story, he "burned with anger against the man." The king declared, "As surely as the LORD lives, the man who did this must die!"

David knew the rich man had acted unjustly. Imagine how he felt when Nathan said, "You are the man." Like the rich farmer, David took a woman named Bathsheba, committed adultery, had her husband killed, and then married her. That was the ugly truth revealed to David by Nathan's story. But the king responded in repentance: "I have sinned against the LORD."

Speaking truth can be hard, but when a king needed truth, God sent a truth-speaker. Learn truth. Share truth. Love those who need truth.

SCRIPTURES QUOTED: 2 SAMUEL 12:1, 5, 13

VISION WITHOUT VISION

*Thy word is true from the beginning: and every one of
thy righteous judgments endureth for ever.*

PSALM 119:160 KJV

Blind from a very young age, Fanny Crosby had no memory of seeing a Bible. Before reaching adulthood, she memorized many books of the Bible and prayed, "Teach me thy way, O LORD; I will walk in thy truth."

God's truth hidden in the heart of a blind woman left Fanny to say, "If I had a choice, I would still choose to remain blind. . .for when I die, the first face I will ever see will be the face of my blessed Savior."

Truth was important to Fanny. She understood that "every word of God is pure." As the author of more than nine thousand hymns, Fanny became intimate with truth.

One day a composer visited Fanny. He'd written music but no words for his hymn, and he was to leave in thirty minutes. When Fanny heard the music, she told him that it seemed to say, "Safe in the arms of Jesus." The composer left with a completed hymn that many still sing today. Fanny's mind and heart were saturated with God's truth that spilled out in her poetic hymns.

Being blind was not Fanny's best life. She was wise enough to realize something much better was coming. The last thing Fanny wrote at the age of ninety-four was "You will reach the river brink, some sweet day, bye and bye."

SCRIPTURES QUOTED: PSALM 86:11; PROVERBS 30:5

PEACE SHOES

*For shoes, put on the peace that comes from the
Good News so that you will be fully prepared.*
EPHESIANS 6:15 NLT

How can you stand firm if you're shaking in worry boots? God wants you to be confident, and not because He thinks you're an action movie warrior. Be confident because you've been given the tools to stand while God declares final victory. Your confidence comes from God's ability not yours.

Hard days become easier when you wear peace shoes—emotional moments are smoother and emergencies less stressful. Your peace flows from the knowledge that God is your rescuer. The Good News is Jesus and everything He finished for you. You can stand tremble-free when your peace is assured. Jesus was clear: "I give them eternal life, and they will never perish. No one can snatch them away from me, for my Father has given them to me, and he is more powerful than anyone else. No one can snatch them from the Father's hand."

The idea of peace shoes is not a passing notion. Paul offered this blessing to the people in Thessalonica: "Now may the Lord of peace himself give you his peace at all times and in every situation. The Lord be with you all." And D. L. Moody said, "There cannot be any peace where there is uncertainty." Be sure in Jesus and discover unfailing peace.

There's no need to feel alone in the battle. God is with you.

SCRIPTURES QUOTED: JOHN 10:28–29; 2 THESSALONIANS 3:16

PEACE PROTECTION

Hezekiah trusted in the LORD, the God of Israel. There was no one like him among all the kings of Judah, either before him or after him.

2 KINGS 18:5 NIV

Some might argue that David or Solomon was the godliest king in the history of Israel and Judah, but God's Word says it was Hezekiah. His name might be familiar, but what made him so memorable? He had undivided trust in God.

Hezekiah's first claim to fame was that "he held fast to the LORD and did not stop following him." This king "kept the commands the LORD had given Moses." Best of all, "the LORD was with him." That may be why "he was successful in whatever he undertook."

He led Judah faithfully and removed the foreign gods the people had been following. Then his peace was tested when Assyrian soldiers invaded. Their leader declared that God was not big enough to save the people from destruction.

Hezekiah's first response wasn't to inspect his soldiers and finalize battle plans. It wasn't to hide. He prayed to the God of peace. He finished the prayer with a specific request: "Deliver us. . .so that all the kingdoms of the earth may know that you alone, LORD, are God."

And God answered: "I will defend this city." No shaking boots, no uncertainty, and no retreat. God made a promise, and it was enough for the king. He stood firm—in peace shoes.

SCRIPTURES QUOTED: 2 KINGS 18:6, 7; 19:19, 34

STAND-FAST STRENGTH

He that is slow to wrath is of great understanding.
PROVERBS 14:29 KJV

Former NFL coach Tony Dungy refers to his way of engaging with life as "quiet strength." God calls it peace.

As a coach, Tony didn't yell at players. He believed they'd respond to a more measured response. His style of coaching has been adopted by many coaches who worked under him over the years.

Tony had a relatively short career as a professional football player, but his coaching became legendary in team building, success, and quiet strength. He was ranked among the top fifteen personalities most liked by the American public. That put him in the company of people like Tom Hanks and Morgan Freeman. He wasn't looking for this honor, but it does speak to his stand-fast strength.

Tony follows the biblical admonition to "let the peace of God rule in your hearts, to the which also ye are called in one body; and be ye thankful."

Peace and worry make horrible roommates. Here's some more advice from the apostle Paul: "In every thing by prayer and supplication with thanksgiving let your requests be made known unto God. And the peace of God, which passeth all understanding, shall keep your hearts and minds through Christ Jesus."

Peace shoes don't waste tread by running away from the adversary. Instead, those who have experienced God's peace are content to wait to see what God will do next. Peace shoes are a visual reminder that no matter what anyone thinks, God is in control. He always has been.

SCRIPTURES QUOTED: COLOSSIANS 3:15; PHILIPPIANS 4:6–7

*In addition to all of these, hold up the shield of
faith to stop the fiery arrows of the devil.*
EPHESIANS 6:16 NLT

The armor of God isn't complete without a shield representing complete trust in the God who crafted each piece of armor. Never doubt that God's hardware is customized specifically for your needs—in fact, each piece *exceeds* any need you may have. Each piece is designed for your protection from the enemy's schemes, so don't be caught unprepared.

Satan wants to destroy you, and he takes aim at your life with deadly accuracy. He revels in your destruction. The faith shield God offers shelters you from enemy fire. But you have to use it. God doesn't want you to trust "in human wisdom but in the power of God." So don't try to stand up to the devil in your own strength or you'll be overwhelmed. Instead "live by believing."

When your faith falters, you've set your shield aside and invited God's enemy to use you for target practice. God has given you divine protection. There's no need to invent new ways that weren't authored by God. His instructions are for your benefit, not to be dismissed as outdated. God doesn't have an expiration date or change with the times. He hasn't moved to a celestial nursing home. So don't expose yourself to the enemy—have faith and take up your shield.

SCRIPTURES QUOTED: 1 CORINTHIANS 2:5; 2 CORINTHIANS 5:7

NEW LEADER—SAME GOD

*These were all commended for their faith, yet none of them received what
had been promised, since God had planned something better for us
so that only together with us would they be made perfect.*

HEBREWS 11:39—40 NIV

Moses was Joshua's mentor. The younger man stood ringside for all the petty
battles Moses faced with the wilderness-weary Israelites. But Moses wouldn't
lead the people into the Promised Land. That honor belonged to Joshua.

Joshua had the faith needed to believe, in spite of the difficulties he
would face, that God could be trusted to figure out how to bring His people
home to the land He'd promised.

God assured Joshua, "As I was with Moses, so I will be with you; I will
never leave you nor forsake you." This new leader grew up a slave in Egypt,
he'd wandered forty years in the wilderness, and he'd witnessed the rebellion of the people. But he also trusted the God who wasn't going anywhere.

Joshua trusted God with the lives of more than a million wanderers. He
faced opposition, complaints, and disputes, but Joshua famously stated his
case for following God: "If serving the LORD seems undesirable to you, then
choose for yourselves this day whom you will serve. . . . As for me and my
household, we will serve the LORD."

Moses didn't enter the Promised Land, but a life of determining borders
and settling disputes was nothing compared to his eternal future. And Joshua
would one day joyfully follow his mentor into that better day.

SCRIPTURES QUOTED: JOSHUA 1:5, 24:15

WAR WOUNDS

*The beloved of the Lord shall dwell in safety by him; and the Lord shall cover
him all the day long, and he shall dwell between his shoulders.*

DEUTERONOMY 33:12 KJV

Darlene Deibler and her husband, Russell, picked the worst time, humanly
speaking, to become missionaries to Papua New Guinea. Darlene was the
first American woman to visit the Baliem Valley. At first, the people didn't
believe she was human. They were suspicious because they'd never seen
anything like her. The couple's faith sustained them in those early days as
they discovered success. Darlene needed God's strength even more when
World War II arrived on the shores of Papua New Guinea.

Japanese soldiers took Russell to one prison camp and Darlene to another.
For four years God's faith shield was Darlene's constant companion. Beaten
and surviving on porridge polluted with worms, rats, and birds that fell into
the pot, she grew thin and weak and suffered with disease.

She waited three months to learn that her husband had died in the
prison camp, yet for more than four decades Darlene stayed and served.
She lived the prayer "I have trusted in thy mercy; my heart shall rejoice
in thy salvation." She wore the wounds of war, but she knew that the most
difficult experience she faced on earth would be amply rewarded in heaven.
"Provide yourselves. . .a treasure in the heavens that faileth not, where no
thief approacheth, neither moth corrupteth. For where your treasure is,
there will your heart be also."

SCRIPTURES QUOTED: PSALM 13:5; LUKE 12:33–34

HELMET OF SALVATION

Put on salvation as your helmet.
EPHESIANS 6:17 NLT

A soldier's helmet protects the head and by extension the mind. If you're without a helmet, the enemy knows he can attack what you think.

God's helmet of salvation turns back the enemy's lies. Satan would have you question the goodness of God, your commander in chief. If your mind isn't protected against these blows, you might conclude God's goodness is a fable. Soldiers need to remember that they've been rescued and what they've been rescued from. They need to remember they've been rescued for a purpose: "Not because of the righteous things we had done, but because of his mercy. He washed away our sins, giving us a new birth and new life through the Holy Spirit."

The helmet protects your mind by reminding you of God's Great Rescue. And the name of Jesus is your salvation: "There is salvation in no one else! God has given no other name under heaven by which we must be saved."

The devil delights in introducing doubt to unprotected minds. If he can convince you that God is not good, you'll inevitably doubt His motives. . .so protect your mind.

SCRIPTURES QUOTED: TITUS 3:5; ACTS 4:12

NIC BY NIGHT

Jesus replied, "Very truly I tell you, no one can see the kingdom of God unless they are born again." "How can someone be born when they are old?" Nicodemus asked.

JOHN 3:3–4 NIV

Nicodemus was a Pharisee, a member of the Jewish ruling council. This religious group believed that no one could follow God as well as they could, and they had a track record of singing their own praises and seeing others as inferior.

Jesus caught the attention of Nicodemus. Something about what Jesus taught made sense to this particular Pharisee. Nicodemus wanted to know more about salvation, so he came at night and spent time with Jesus. The Pharisee began by honoring Jesus: "Rabbi, we know that you are a teacher who has come from God. For no one could perform the signs you are doing if God were not with him." Could a Pharisee actually follow Jesus?

The Pharisees had received harsh words from Jesus, but in this conversation with Nicodemus, Jesus said, "God did not send his Son into the world to condemn the world, but to save the world through him." Rescue was something even a Pharisee could experience. The Pharisees tried to earn God's favor by following the letter of the law because they thought the law could deliver them. They believed a lie, and it affected every area of their lives.

But salvation came through another source—Jesus—for all who recognize their sin and reach out for His rescue.

SCRIPTURES QUOTED: JOHN 3:2, 17

NO BOAST, NO BRAG

For by grace are ye saved through faith; and that not of yourselves:
it is the gift of God: Not of works, lest any man should boast.

EPHESIANS 2:8—9 KJV

Bragging accentuates your strengths, but it also causes other people to feel weaker and inferior. Some think that their great success proves that God loves them just a little bit more than most.

Louis Zamperini's experiences would make an impressive highlight reel. He didn't speak English in his early school years and was raised under difficult circumstances, yet he achieved remarkable things. He became an Olympic athlete and as a member of the US military survived both a month adrift on the ocean and being a prisoner of war.

If you could earn a spot in heaven based on what you've lived through, then Louis would make a good candidate—but you can't. Jesus said, "I am the way, the truth, and the life: no man cometh unto the Father, but by me."

Louis endured the most difficult moments of his life outside a relationship with Jesus. But it was God's salvation that changed his thinking. There was no reason for boasting, bragging, or conceit. Louis needed forgiveness, and he needed to learn to forgive. He'd trusted in his ability to endure, but Louis needed to trust the God who'd given him a new family. "But as many as received him, to them gave he power to become the sons of God, even to them that believe on his name."

Salvation changes your thinking. Boast only in Jesus' victory.

SCRIPTURES QUOTED: JOHN 14:6, 1:12

THE SPIRIT'S SWORD

Take the sword of the Spirit, which is the word of God.
EPHESIANS 6:17 NLT

Put on each piece of God's armor carefully, deliberately, and with purpose because the enemy is on the attack. He's hoping you don't know what God says so he can lead you to believe a sweet-sounding lie.

God's Word isn't an ornament or a spiritual good-luck charm. It's a battle plan that leads to victory over the enemy. "Be prepared, whether the time is favorable or not. Patiently correct, rebuke, and encourage. . .with good teaching."

Every other piece of armor is designed for defense, but the sword of the Spirit is an offensive weapon. Jesus wielded it effectively when tempted in the wilderness, and you too can use it to counter wrong thinking. "You say you have faith, for you believe that there is one God. Good for you! Even the demons believe this, and they tremble in terror." The devil knows scripture, but he has no problem taking things out of context as he tries to use God's words to confuse you. He knows he'll ultimately lose, but that never stops him from trying to take you down with him. He'll try again today.

Learn God's Word. It's the only way to discern truth from this world's lies.

SCRIPTURES QUOTED: 2 TIMOTHY 4:2; JAMES 2:19

TEACHING TIMOTHY

For I am not ashamed of the gospel, because it is the power of God that brings
salvation to everyone who believes: first to the Jew, then to the Gentile.
ROMANS 1:16 NIV

Timothy was part of a growing group who'd discovered good news in God's
Word. Most people believed God was only for Jews, but Jesus taught that
salvation was available to anyone.

Timothy was mentored by the apostle Paul, and learning God's Word was
his greatest priority. He was given great responsibility in the leadership of
the early church. Paul had specific instructions for this young man: "Continue in what you have learned and have become convinced of. . .and how
from infancy you have known the Holy Scriptures, which are able to make
you wise for salvation through faith in Christ Jesus."

Paul's words reminded Timothy to wear the helmet of salvation and always
carry the sword of God's Spirit. Successful Christians are always covered by
their armor. Don't fall for the lie that once you've followed God long enough,
your armor isn't necessary. This thinking always leads to days of defeat.

Paul reminded Timothy that there was a better day coming. "Train
yourself to be godly. For physical training is of some value, but godliness
has value for all things, holding promise for both the present life and the
life to come."

God came for you—to rescue, train, and prepare you for the temporary
suffering you would have faced even if you hadn't been rescued. Now, you
have help.

SCRIPTURES QUOTED: 2 TIMOTHY 3:14—15; 1 TIMOTHY 4:7—8

SIMPLE, YET PROFOUND

For the word of God is quick, and powerful, and sharper than any twoedged sword, piercing even to the dividing asunder of soul and spirit, and of the joints and marrow, and is a discerner of the thoughts and intents of the heart.

HEBREWS 4:12 KJV

Billy Graham started his ministry with a simple idea that sustained him through decades of ministry. He made the Bible central to everything he taught, and the most important topic in his messages was God's offer of rescue.

Billy preached to 2.5 *billion* people and led 3.2 *million* to Jesus. Eleven US presidents considered Billy their spiritual advisor.

But Billy wasn't primarily interested in statistics. He wanted people to know that they *could* be saved and experience a relationship with God: "For ye are all the children of God by faith in Christ Jesus."

Billy defended God's good news despite what others thought and earned a reputation for integrity, obedience, and grace by following scripture. Billy knew that "the law of the LORD is perfect, converting the soul: the testimony of the LORD is sure, making wise the simple."

Billy's simple message was backed by God's profound wisdom. Billy asked and God provided. This is a prayer God wants to fulfill. If you are seeking wisdom, pray and ask your heavenly Father, and He will teach you His unfailing wisdom.

SCRIPTURES QUOTED: GALATIANS 3:26; PSALM 19:7

JOY VERSUS HAPPINESS

You love him even though you have never seen him. Though you do not see him now, you trust him; and you rejoice with a glorious, inexpressible joy.

1 PETER 1:8 NLT

Happiness is a fickle emotion that seems to show up only when something good happens. Happiness can bloom in your heart for purely selfish gains—the economy is good, you finally check something off your bucket list, or even because someone said they liked you.

But when the economy isn't so great, health issues prevent you from doing the thing you've always wanted to do, or friends abandon you, happiness seems to flee as well. To find joy in each moment, you have to accept God's promise of a better day to come.

Scripture says, "When troubles of any kind come your way, consider it an opportunity for great joy. For you know that when your faith is tested, your endurance has a chance to grow. So let it grow, for when your endurance is fully developed, you will be perfect and complete, needing nothing."

Joy is the byproduct of a close relationship with God. Your troubles can offer the precious gift of witnessing God's faithfulness. As you experience His faithfulness, your trust in the God who loves you will twine deep into your soul, and you will know for certain there's a better day coming. Whatever happens today is but a minor inconvenience when compared to what God has promised.

Don't make fleeting happiness your first pursuit. Joy will last forever because its source springs from our eternal God.

SCRIPTURES QUOTED: JAMES 1:2—4

THE JOYFUL DAUGHTER-IN-LAW

Ruth replied, "Don't urge me to leave you or to turn back from
you. Where you go I will go, and where you stay I will stay.
Your people will be my people and your God my God."

RUTH 1:16 NIV

Ruth suffered the death of her husband, brother-in-law, and father-in-law. She endured enough grief to last a lifetime, and she wanted something different. She sought joy.

After her husband's death, her mother-in-law encouraged her to return home to her parents, but instead Ruth chose to follow Naomi back to Israel. When they arrived, "the barley harvest was beginning."

There were no jobs waiting for the widows. Naomi stayed home while Ruth took advantage of a law that allowed foreigners and widows to glean the leftover grain from the harvested fields.

This wasn't a happy life for Ruth, but she was learning the value of joy and where to find it. She could trust God to give her a future she thought impossible. By trusting God, Ruth gained a new husband, Boaz, and a son, Obed. And God's plan unfurled in spectacular glory when Ruth's great-grandson David became king.

Ruth discovered joy in an unlikely place, but she had witnessed miracles. She told her mother-in-law, "May the LORD deal with me, be it ever so severely, if even death separates you and me." Following God's directions always presents a fresh opportunity to be inspired by joy.

SCRIPTURES QUOTED: RUTH 1:22, 17

JOY AFTER PAIN

Ye now therefore have sorrow: but I will see you again, and your heart shall rejoice, and your joy no man taketh from you.

JOHN 16:22 KJV

When you believe that God has an amazing eternal future planned for you, choosing joy becomes much easier. But don't confuse happiness with joy because there are some differences.

Chonda Pierce is a Christian comedian. She makes people happy whenever she steps onto the stage. But her own life has been filled with moments of unhappiness. Often the most humorous people have endured the greatest pain.

Chonda has enjoyed opportunities to sing, act, and do stand-up comedy. Yet her two sisters died before reaching adulthood. Her husband faced addiction and then he also died, and she's estranged from her daughter. But joy connects to the eternal, while happiness is a limited and momentary escape from today.

Joy comes from the heart of God. "Let all those that put their trust in thee rejoice: let them ever shout for joy, because thou defendest them: let them also that love thy name be joyful in thee."

God's joy is not dependent on your past, and it has nothing to do with present circumstances. But the future hope of God's better day can bring you face-to-face with joy. You can exist with that joy today. You don't need to wait.

If you struggle with your past or can't see beyond today, consider this biblical prayer: "Restore unto me the joy of thy salvation; and uphold me with thy free spirit."

SCRIPTURES QUOTED: PSALM 5:11, 51:12

LIVING NEW

Anyone who belongs to Christ has become a new person.
The old life is gone; a new life has begun!
2 CORINTHIANS 5:17 NLT

Sin found a home when Adam and Eve disobeyed God, and physical death was assured when God said, "For you were made from dust, and to dust you will return."

But don't be discouraged. Death isn't final. Death serves only as a reminder that you need to prepare *now* for what's next. Even Bugs Bunny knew that "no one gets out alive." Your best day on earth will seem dim compared to the glorious eternal future that awaits—no more pain, no death, no separation from God or those we love. Every evil will be wiped out and every injustice corrected.

If that doesn't sound attractive, maybe you need to adjust your perspective. When life here becomes more important than being forever in the presence of God, we lose our spiritual vision.

On earth we make the most important choice of our lives—accept Jesus or reject Him. Become a new creation now to prepare for your better day to come. Reject your old ways—the life that would separate you from God forever.

"My old self has been crucified with Christ. It is no longer I who live, but Christ lives in me. So I live in this earthly body by trusting in the Son of God, who loved me and gave himself for me." That's the bold declaration of one who understands there is more to life than what happens today. Are you ready for the better day to come?

SCRIPTURES QUOTED: GENESIS 3:19; GALATIANS 2:20

HE DIDN'T KNOW IT ALL

Pride brings a person low, but the lowly in spirit gain honor.
PROVERBS 29:23 NIV

Peter was a my-dad's-tougher-than-your-dad kind of guy. He liked to brag, made promises he couldn't keep, and was brash and bold. He was larger than life and desperately wanted to be teacher's pet.

He was more impulsive than the rest of the disciples combined, yet Peter was certain he did *not* have a problem, even when Jesus pointed it out. But Jesus still had plans for this hotheaded man of knee-jerk decisions. "You are Peter, and on this rock I will build my church."

It might seem counterintuitive to suggest a hotheaded disciple would build a church. But Jesus saw his potential for God's kingdom if Peter embraced a new way of living—and He knew something about Peter that others didn't. Peter would release pride for humility and admit he didn't know it all. He wouldn't settle for being what he'd always been. As Peter would later write, "All of you, be like-minded, be sympathetic, love one another, be compassionate and humble. Do not repay evil with evil or insult with insult."

Jesus saw something in Peter that even Peter didn't see. The same potential is what He sees in you. What He offers isn't an extreme makeover, it's something entirely new. It's not upcycling, it's the beginning of something different. It's not reconstructive surgery, it's freshly minted life.

Stop trying to clean yourself up first—ask for His new life now.

SCRIPTURES QUOTED: MATTHEW 16:18; 1 PETER 3:8—9

JOHN, THE WRETCH

Be not conformed to this world: but be ye transformed by the renewing of your mind, that ye may prove what is that good, and acceptable, and perfect, will of God.

ROMANS 12:2 KJV

John Newton was an eighteenth-century slave trader. Men, women, and children endured an agonizing voyage from Africa to England aboard his ship. But in the midst of a violent storm, John began to reconsider his life choices. He realized the God of his childhood could never support the evil of human bondage as the slaves' songs cried out to him.

John's prayer likely mirrored this: "Create in me a clean heart, O God; and renew a right spirit within me."

He dedicated his life to God and penned a few hundred hymns. One of his most famous referred to sinners as wretches. That's how John thought of himself before God rescued him through His "Amazing Grace."

John was right to see himself as a sinner, to ask God to "see if there be any wicked way in me, and lead me in the way everlasting," and to seek freedom for the captives. Shortly after slavery was abolished in England in 1807, John stepped forward into his better day. He had experienced God's amazing grace—and it was enough.

SCRIPTURES QUOTED: PSALM 51:10, 139:24

[God] gives grace generously. As the Scriptures say,
"God opposes the proud but gives grace to the humble."
JAMES 4:6 NLT

People describe grace in many ways. Its simplest definition may be, "Jesus loves me, this I know." In practice, grace is getting everything God has for you even though you don't deserve it.

That may be why some people think they should have whatever they want. That's grace, right? Grace admits you to God's family, makes you a child of God, and gives you a future with Him. Some things you have access to now, and some you will have to wait for. Other things you *think* God wants for you may have never been in His plan, so don't complain. God isn't a fan of demands or tantrums.

Grace isn't a blank check to get what you want. It's a preview of coming attractions. It's a mental and spiritual album you fill when the only possible explanation is that not only did God show up, but He brought a miracle—and you saw it firsthand.

God's grace is a big deal: "For the grace of God has been revealed, bringing salvation to all people. And we are instructed to turn from godless living and sinful pleasures. We should live in this evil world with wisdom, righteousness, and devotion to God."

Accept God's grace, be amazed by it—but don't turn it into something God never said it was.

SCRIPTURES QUOTED: TITUS 2:11–12

VIEW FROM THE SYCAMORE

Zacchaeus stood up and said to the Lord, "Look, Lord! Here and now I give half of my possessions to the poor, and if I have cheated anybody out of anything, I will pay back four times the amount."
LUKE 19:8 NIV

In the modern world, we can watch something important on TV, live stream the event, or wait for it to show up on social media—without ever leaving the comfort of our favorite recliner. For Zacchaeus, none of these options were available. Jesus was coming to his neighborhood, and Zacchaeus needed to see what he had only heard about. "He wanted to see who Jesus was, but because he was short he could not see over the crowd. So he ran ahead and climbed a sycamore-fig tree to see him."

He picked a good spot. He saw Jesus—then Jesus saw him. "Zacchaeus, come down immediately. I must stay at your house today." Jesus was God's Son, creator of everything. He knew no strangers.

Zacchaeus was a rich tax collector. He earned his wealth by overcharging the people and skimming the excess for himself. Then he met grace. His trust had been misplaced, but that was before Jesus said that He, the Son of Man, "came to seek and to save the lost."

Zacchaeus was awestruck in that sycamore tree. In the presence of God's grace, he captured a snapshot of something better—something that changed his life—something undeserved and overwhelmingly priceless. He experienced grace.

SCRIPTURES QUOTED: LUKE 19:3–4, 5, 10

REJECTED BUT REDEEMED

We have redemption through his blood, the forgiveness of sins,
according to the riches of his grace.

EPHESIANS 1:7 KJV

God doesn't judge you for the actions of your parents. And He didn't judge William J. Murray by the actions of his mother, Madalyn Murray O'Hair, either.

Some people grow up in homes where Jesus is welcome and being a Christian is a valued life choice. But William's mom was an atheist. She did whatever she could to silence Christian voices. She lobbied until most public prayer and Bible reading in school was eliminated.

But in spite of his upbringing, William became a Christian in his midthirties. His mom was not pleased by the news: "I repudiate him entirely and completely for now and all times. He is beyond human forgiveness."

While William would have welcomed human forgiveness, he was after something more precious—divine forgiveness and a friendship with God. William discovered a spiritual family that loved him, accepted his adoption, and welcomed him wholeheartedly. This atheist's son became a pastor. With all the obstacles William faced, his life echoed this biblical truth: "None of these things move me, neither count I my life dear unto myself, so that I might finish my course with joy, and the ministry, which I have received of the Lord Jesus, to testify the gospel of the grace of God."

New life begins with an undeserved God gift that you fully believe is yours. The steps you take today lead you closer to that eternal better day.

SCRIPTURES QUOTED: ACTS 20:24

MERCIFUL GOODNESS

There will be no mercy for those who have not shown mercy to others.
But if you have been merciful, God will be merciful when he judges you.

JAMES 2:13 NLT

Mercy is rooted in love, kindness, and compassion. It doesn't discount sin or say it doesn't matter. Mercy sees the person behind the mistake. It recognizes failure but believes in restoration. It seeks to be kind because it is kind.

Mercy doesn't look for happiness in the misfortune of others. Mercy believes in reaching out to help others not push them down or away. When others don't see mercy in you, they will likely withhold mercy when you could use some. Have you heard of the Golden Rule? "Do to others as you would like them to do to you."

Mercy recognizes your mistakes but wants you to see the face of a friend before a court date. God is just and will set things right, but between now and then kindness might change a few things justice can't. "Don't you see how wonderfully kind, tolerant, and patient God is with you? Does this mean nothing to you? Can't you see that his kindness is intended to turn you from your sin?"

Let mercy lend a listening ear, a strong shoulder to cry on, and kind acceptance. Your better day to come will be lived in the company of the God who created mercy, shows mercy, and asks you to be merciful.

SCRIPTURES QUOTED: LUKE 6:31; ROMANS 2:4

SECONDHAND MERCY

[Nabal asked], "Why should I take my bread and water, and the
meat I have slaughtered for my shearers, and give it to
men coming from who knows where?"

1 SAMUEL 25:11 NIV

Maybe wealth contributed to the meanness that rattled Nabal's bones. He had more than he needed but couldn't be bothered to help others—not even a man who had shown him kindness.

David was the future king, and while he waited, he protected men like Nabal and their possessions from attack.

It was a time of festival, and David wanted to celebrate with the men who followed Him. He sent a message to Nabal: "Be favorable toward my men, since we come at a festive time. Please give your servants and your son David whatever you can find for them."

David didn't ask to see a menu. He didn't ask for anything special to be prepared. He hoped his mercy would be recognized and returned, but it wasn't.

Anger warred within David and temporarily won. He prepared for battle against the miserly Nabal. But secondhand mercy stopped the war. Nabal's wife, Abigail, loaded several donkeys with food and found David. "Let this gift, which your servant has brought to my lord, be given to the men who follow you."

You can almost imagine David releasing a sigh of relief. War was avoided at just the right time. David looked at Abigail and said, "Go home in peace."

Peace and mercy are always preferred to personal war and judgment.

SCRIPTURES QUOTED: 1 SAMUEL 25:8, 27, 35

HE MET MERCY

Blessed are the merciful: for they shall obtain mercy.
MATTHEW 5:7 KJV

He was declared stillborn. The medical staff moved their attention to the mother. For nearly twenty minutes the baby boy lay dead. Then miraculously, David Ring somehow, against all odds, lived. But prolonged oxygen deprivation left him suffering from cerebral palsy and lifelong physical limitations. Walking and talking would present a challenge.

His mother modeled mercy for him, and it was his first glimpse at something birthed in the heart of God.

But David was orphaned at age fourteen. He dropped out of school and attempted suicide. People made fun of him. Then God reintroduced him to mercy, and it changed him. "It is of the LORD's mercies that we are not consumed, because his compassions fail not. They are new every morning: great is thy faithfulness."

David didn't think he would ever get married or become a father, but not only does he have a wife and four children, he also speaks to large crowds. He even sings in a way only he can.

Mercy? Perhaps David said it best, "God. . .why were you so good to me?"

David sings an emotional version of "Victory in Jesus." He remembers a broken past and can sing with the psalmist, "Remember not the sins of my youth, nor my transgressions: according to thy mercy remember thou me for thy goodness' sake, O LORD." And on his better day to come, David will be whole and see mercy face-to-face.

SCRIPTURES QUOTED: LAMENTATIONS 3:22–23; PSALM 25:7

GOD DOESN'T SECOND GUESS

"I am the Alpha and the Omega—the beginning and the end,"
says the Lord God. "I am the one who is, who always
was, and who is still to come—the Almighty One."

REVELATION 1:8 NLT

Understanding who God is can help you see why life here is a distant second to heaven. You have a birthday, but God has always been. You will one day die, but God always will be. You have days of weakness, but God is the Almighty One. This piece of good news will never change.

God boldly declared, "I am the LORD, the God of all the peoples of the world. Is anything too hard for me?" The question needs no answer—nothing is too hard for God. He is bigger than your greatest failure, your health problems, losing your job, or even your tough relationships.

He has the answers you seek. God lives with no regrets, no second guesses, no wrong decisions. Nothing escapes His attention or surprises Him. That's why you can say, "When I look at the night sky and see the work of your fingers—the moon and the stars you set in place—what are mere mortals that you should think about them, human beings that you should care for them?"

God is infinite and He is good. This almighty God wants to deliver a better day that will be much better than your best so far.

SCRIPTURES QUOTED: JEREMIAH 32:27; PSALM 8:3–4

NEEDS, AND A KNOWING GOD

Then one of the synagogue leaders, named Jairus, came, and when he saw Jesus, he fell at his feet. He pleaded earnestly with him, "My little daughter is dying. Please come and put your hands on her so that she will be healed and live." So Jesus went with him.

MARK 5:22–24 NIV

It was a busy day for Jesus. The crowds were large, needs were great, and compassion was the common hope. Jesus had been asked to come and heal a young girl, but the needs of the crowd delayed him. When He was finally on His way, sad news arrived for the little girl's father. "Your daughter is dead. Why bother the teacher anymore?" But Jesus said, "Don't be afraid; just believe."

The crowd thought it was ridiculous when Jesus said, "The child is not dead but asleep." So Jesus followed the parents into the room where the girl lay. He held her hand and said, "Little girl, I say to you, get up!" The girl, once dead, lived. Who but the Son of God could do this? God is well acquainted with beginnings and ends—He can bring life out of death. And His purpose extends beyond our earthly death.

But knowing God doesn't always mean you know exactly what He will do. Those who think God is predictable are often proven wrong because He sees the world on a scale we can never comprehend. Instead of trying to force your plans on God, trust Him to know the best path.

SCRIPTURES QUOTED: MARK 5:35, 36, 39, 41

GOD'S ADVENTURE

Great is our Lord, and of great power: his understanding is infinite.
PSALM 147:5 KJV

Jim Elliot's life was ended by the spear of an elusive tribe of Ecuadorian Indians. To many people, the news made little sense. Jim and four of his missionary friends were trying to tell the people about Jesus. But this wasn't the end of God's plan.

Jim grew up in a strong Christian family who believed in following God's big adventure. Jim served an infinite God. He once said, "Forgive me for being so ordinary while claiming to know so extraordinary a God."

Jim knew that being a missionary could be dangerous, but because of the adventure God birthed in Jim's heart, he said, "He is no fool who gives what he cannot keep to gain that which he cannot lose."

God is full of surprises: "him that is able to do exceeding abundantly above all that we ask or think," according to the apostle Paul. He does more than you ask or think, but He may do it differently than you expect. While it may not make sense for one of God's servants to die, in God's infinite wisdom, Jim exited the great adventure in favor of his better day. "The LORD thy God in the midst of thee is mighty; he will save, he will rejoice over thee with joy; he will rest in his love, he will joy over thee with singing."

SCRIPTURES QUOTED: EPHESIANS 3:20; ZEPHANIAH 3:17

CHANGELESS

"I am the Lord, and I do not change."
MALACHI 3:6 NLT

There is comfort in knowing God doesn't change—He's steady, solid, and dependable. But it also means that His truth doesn't change, waver, or require a makeover.

Sometimes we find truth in scripture that we don't want to believe, words we think are for someone else. We might even convince ourselves that the Bible should be condensed so only the encouraging bits remain, but "the word of the Lord remains forever." Don't confuse God's mercy with a relaxed standard. The first is a gift, and the second suggests God could alter His expectations.

Scripture says, "Your eternal word, O Lord, stands firm in heaven." God doesn't change, nor does His Word. And His love for you doesn't change either.

But we do change. We break promises, and our love for others grows tepid. This is why God works within us to make us into a new creation. Charles Spurgeon said, "Though you have changed a thousand times, He has not changed once."

We need preparation for our better day, and that doesn't happen without His help. Let the God who never changes change you. Allow Him to renew your thinking, actions, and beliefs. Pray that each day you would look more and more like the God who never changes.

SCRIPTURES QUOTED: 1 PETER 1:25; PSALM 119:89

RELIABLY TRANSFORMED

Barnabas wanted to take John, also called Mark, with them, but Paul did not think it wise to take him, because he had deserted them in Pamphylia and had not continued with them in the work.

ACTS 15:37–38 NIV

Any missionary journey takes planning and preparation. It may also involve danger and difficulty. Most missionaries work with people they trust, people with a solid reputation who won't let them down.

John Mark wanted a new adventure. He'd accompanied Paul and Barnabas on a mission trip before, but this time they were hesitant to trust him because he'd left before the work was done. So Paul didn't want him along.

Paul had visited John Mark's family who hosted fellow Christians in their home in Jerusalem. He knew the family, but more importantly he knew the God who can change a person. The Bible may not be clear about what changed for John Mark, but Paul would eventually say, "Get Mark and bring him with you, because he is helpful to me in my ministry."

God changed this young man from deserter to reliable companion. In fact, it's believed he was used by God to write the Gospel of Mark.

The Bible is clear that John Mark had a family connection to Barnabas, "My fellow prisoner Aristarchus sends you his greetings, as does Mark, the cousin of Barnabas. (You have received instructions about him; if he comes to you, welcome him.)"

Welcome him? Things *had* changed for John Mark, and God did the changing.

SCRIPTURES QUOTED: 2 TIMOTHY 4:11; COLOSSIANS 4:10

PROVING GOD WRONG?
THE IMPOSSIBLE QUEST

God is not a man, that he should lie; neither the son of man,
that he should repent: hath he said, and shall he not do it?
or hath he spoken, and shall he not make it good?

NUMBERS 23:19 KJV

Lee Strobel was among the best and brightest. He was an award-winning journalist with an impressive background. Lee had gone to Yale, worked for the Chicago *Tribune*, and had the hardware in his trophy chest.

But Lee hated God.

His antagonism may have impressed some people, but perhaps others prayed for him. After Lee's wife, Leslie, became a Christian, he began to use his investigative journalist background to investigate God. As an atheist, could God prove anything to him?

Lee's journey can be summed up in scripture: "The heart of the prudent getteth knowledge; and the ear of the wise seeketh knowledge." Lee had knowledge, but he lacked wisdom.

As Lee pored over God's Word, his bright mind detected what he'd hoped to avoid—wisdom and truth. And God's truth led to a change in Lee.

God birthed something new out of hate: "The Lord is not slack concerning his promise, as some men count slackness; but is longsuffering to us-ward, not willing that any should perish, but that all should come to repentance."

Today, Lee is an apologist. He defends the truth of God's Word whenever someone insists truth doesn't exist. God's truth changed a heart of stone to flesh, and He can bring new life to yours as well.

SCRIPTURES QUOTED: PROVERBS 18:15; 2 PETER 3:9

HIS GLORY

"I am the LORD; that is my name! I will not give my glory to anyone else, nor share my praise with carved idols."
ISAIAH 42:8 NLT

Anytime we do good there's always someone we could thank for our ability to help others—a person who came to our aid in a time of need or someone who taught us a useful skill. But God is not good because of another's example. Instead His goodness stems from His character. So when you say He is glorious, there is no one higher up that He can thank. When you offer praise, the buck stops with Him.

How does the Bible describe God's glory? "His coming is as brilliant as the sunrise. Rays of light flash from his hands, where his awesome power is hidden."

Can you create something more splendid than a white sand beach? Can you orchestrate clouds for the perfect sunset? Can you ask the winds to melt snow for a brilliant waterfall? God does—and it's glorious. "For everything comes from him and exists by his power and is intended for his glory. All glory to him forever! Amen."

Glory can be expressed anywhere. Charles Spurgeon said, "The shop, the barn, the scullery, and the smithy become temples when men and women do all to the glory of God! The 'divine service' is not a thing of a few hours and a few places, but all life becomes holiness unto the Lord, and every place and thing, as consecrated as the tabernacle and its golden candlestick."

Praise God and recognize His brilliant glory.

SCRIPTURES QUOTED: HABAKKUK 3:4; ROMANS 11:36

DOING THE IMPORTANT

As Jesus and his disciples were on their way, he came to a village where a woman named Martha opened her home to him. She had a sister called Mary, who sat at the Lord's feet listening to what he said.

LUKE 10:38—39 NIV

Kids are all different. You might dress them to match, but their temperaments will never line up.

Jesus knew the unique nature of both Mary and Martha. These two sisters lived together in adulthood. Mary wanted to know what Jesus thought. Martha wanted to make sure Jesus had a good meal. They both seem like worthy choices.

When Martha saw that Mary was listening to Jesus instead of helping, she couldn't stand it: "Lord, don't you care that my sister has left me to do the work by myself? Tell her to help me!"

It seemed a reasonable request—one that most hospitable people would understand. But Martha didn't realize she was telling Jesus that His words were less important than the meal. Jesus made sure she had a clear picture of what He thought was valuable: "You are worried and upset about many things, but few things are needed—or indeed only one. Mary has chosen what is better."

Jesus showed Martha what Mary had already discovered—that He was worth praising and His words were worth heeding. His glory was greater than plate presentation.

SCRIPTURES QUOTED: LUKE 10:40, 41—42

GLORY IN SONG

And the Word was made flesh, and dwelt among us, (and we beheld his glory, the glory as of the only begotten of the Father,) full of grace and truth.

JOHN 1:14 KJV

Bill Gaither has gained worldwide fame for his music—but his story harkens back to his homeland of Indiana. In this quiet place, Bill met his wife, made a home, and raised his children. From Indiana, Bill and Gloria discovered God's glory and reflected it in song. The impact went global.

Gloria writes the words and Bill takes care of the music. The two have collaborated on more than seven hundred songs—many of which are well-known hymns.

God has also equipped *you* to take His glory and express it. It's not something only singers and songwriters do. C. S. Lewis wrote, "A man can no more diminish God's glory by refusing to worship Him than a lunatic can put out the sun by scribbling the word 'darkness' on the walls of his cell."

And if you struggle to glorify God, remember "that the sufferings of this present time are not worthy to be compared with the glory which shall be revealed in us."

Bill Gaither has let his "light so shine before men, that they may see. . . good works, and glorify your Father which is in heaven." He's done that one song at a time. How will you reflect God's glory?

SCRIPTURES QUOTED: ROMANS 8:18; MATTHEW 5:16

PERFECTLY HOLY

No one is holy like the LORD! There is no one
besides you; there is no Rock like our God.

1 SAMUEL 2:2 NLT

God is holy—completely set apart, without sin, and untarnished. God said He wants you to "be holy because I am holy." Being holy is a condition of God's grace and your cooperation.

Consider two truths: God is holy without any help, and we are flawed when we refuse His help. Sinclair Ferguson wrote: "God's holiness means He is separate from sin. But holiness in God also means wholeness. God's holiness is His 'God-ness.' It is His being God in all that it means for Him to be God. To meet God in His holiness, therefore, is to be altogether over-whelmed by the discovery that He is God, and not man."

Recognize that God is holy and sin has never been part of what describes Him. Be grateful that He's not like you, but that you can become more like Him. Express joy knowing that God is something other than a flawed human. Enlarge your faith knowing that your better day will bring you face-to-face with God's perfection—and remove you from the presence of all that is unholy.

Moses asked a great question: "Who is like you among the gods, O LORD— glorious in holiness, awesome in splendor, performing great wonders?" No one is like God. No one but God has perfect holiness. No one is more splendid. No one performs the great wonders of a great God. Worship *that* God. Worship His holiness.

SCRIPTURES QUOTED: 1 PETER 1:16; EXODUS 15:11

FAILED HOLINESS

The word of the LORD came to Jonah son of Amittai: "Go to the great city of Nineveh and preach against it, because its wickedness has come up before me." But Jonah ran away from the LORD.

JONAH 1:1—3 NIV

Jonah was visibly flawed. God had a very specific assignment for Jonah, but this prophet's actions said, "No!"

Jonah flat-out refused to be holy or set apart for God's work. He didn't even try. But God wanted something better from Jonah, so He set him up with some respite accommodations in the belly of a big fish, where he could think without distraction. When Jonah reconsidered his response, "the LORD commanded the fish, and it vomited Jonah onto dry land."

God desires holiness for you too. He said, "Those who cleanse themselves. . .will be instruments for special purposes, made holy, useful to the Master and prepared to do any good work."

God had a task for Jonah: to give the ruthless people a message of mercy if they would turn from their evil ways. But Jonah was angry—turns out, he wanted the people of Nineveh to be destroyed. So God asked Jonah, "Is it right for you to be angry?"

An overlooked part of Jonah's story is that a holy God desired to see one of His servants follow Him into holiness through obedience. So take heart, you're not alone in the struggle.

SCRIPTURES QUOTED: JONAH 2:10; 2 TIMOTHY 2:21; JONAH 4:4

SET APART

For such an high priest became us, who is holy, harmless, undefiled,
separate from sinners, and made higher than the heavens.

HEBREWS 7:26 KJV

If someone took the life of your loved one, would you then dedicate your life to loving the killers? You've read three perspectives on this story. This will be the final look.

Jim Elliot and Nate Saint were two of five men killed in Ecuador by Auca Indians. But Jim's wife, Elisabeth, bravely returned to live among the people who took her husband's life. Two Auca women came to live with Elisabeth. They helped her understand why the men in the tribe took such violent action—the men in the tribe feared for their freedom if these outsiders spent time with the tribe.

Perhaps these tribal members recognized that the missionaries were set aside for a purpose, but they were confused about what their arrival meant.

How often do people understand that God is holy, but they're frightened enough to reject Him? Jesus suffered violence and death because people were afraid of what He was set aside to do. "For he hath made him to be sin for us, who knew no sin; that we might be made the righteousness of God in him."

And God has called you for His purpose too: "[God] hath saved us, and called us with an holy calling, not according to our works, but according to his own purpose and grace."

SCRIPTURES QUOTED: 2 CORINTHIANS 5:21; 2 TIMOTHY 1:9

PERFECTLY LOVED

*God showed his great love for us by sending Christ
to die for us while we were still sinners.*

ROMANS 5:8 NLT

It's tough to live our best lives when we're not equipped to love each other perfectly. No human will ever meet your every need or has the ability to love you entirely without conditions. You are probably familiar with a love that carries exception clauses.

But God loves you unconditionally. He loves you perfectly. He even loved you when you were a card-carrying rebel. "This is how God loved the world: He gave his one and only Son, so that everyone who believes in him will not perish but have eternal life."

And while people will betray, leave, or hurt you, be "convinced that nothing can ever separate us from God's love. Neither death nor life, neither angels nor demons, neither our fears for today nor our worries about tomorrow—not even the powers of hell can separate us from God's love. No power in the sky above or in the earth below—indeed, nothing in all creation will ever be able to separate us from the love of God that is revealed in Christ Jesus our Lord."

Being loved perfectly by God is the clarion call to your future better day. It's a perfect "Welcome home!" Why would you need to settle for less? God calls you to His kind of love. He wants you to receive it and share it. He wants you to receive it. No conditions. No exceptions.

SCRIPTURES QUOTED: JOHN 3:16; ROMANS 8:38–39

LOVE'S CURE

Bands of raiders from Aram had gone out and had taken captive a young
girl from Israel, and she served Naaman's wife. She said to her mistress,
"If only my master would see the prophet who is in Samaria!
He would cure him of his leprosy."

2 KINGS 5:2–3 NIV

Naaman wasn't an Israelite. He was suffering from leprosy and impatient
to find a cure.

The king of Israel was frustrated when he read the letter from the
king of Aram. "I am sending my servant Naaman to you so that you may
cure him of his leprosy." The king knew he wasn't God and that only God
could heal the sick. He feared this request could bring war, and he had
no idea how to respond.

That's when the prophet Elisha came into the picture. He sent a messenger to tell Naaman, "Go, wash yourself seven times in the Jordan, and
your flesh will be restored and you will be cleansed."

Naaman wasn't thrilled that Elisha hadn't seen him personally, and he
thought the Jordan River was disgusting. But on the seventh time washing
in the river, Naaman emerged healed and whole.

This healing started with the unconditional love of a kidnapped servant
girl. She cared enough about Naaman to suggest there was healing waiting in
Israel. Her name is never mentioned, and we don't know whether she was
ever released from slavery, but this young lady had been taught that there
was a God who loved people. If anyone could heal her master, it was this God.

SCRIPTURES QUOTED: 2 KINGS 5:6, 10

LOVE DELIVERED

Beloved, let us love one another: for love is of God; and every one that loveth is born of God, and knoweth God. He that loveth not knoweth not God; for God is love.

1 JOHN 4:7—8 KJV

The year was 1968. Missionaries Stan Dale and Phil Masters were on their way to the Snow Mountains in Irian Jaya, Indonesia. The people who lived there had not encountered Jesus, and these missionaries wanted to change that.

In preparation, Stan urged people to "continue to remember us in prayer, for we still carry some heavy burdens."

The Yali were feared, aggressive cannibals who were avoided by other tribes, but Stan and Dale visited the Yali on purpose. Stan had met the Yali once before and escaped with five arrows lodged in his body as their warning to stay away.

Once again the missionaries attempted to deliver God's love, but this time they paid with their lives. As arrows found their mark, these two missionaries could say, "For our light affliction, which is but for a moment, worketh for us a far more exceeding and eternal weight of glory; while we look not at the things which are seen, but at the things which are not seen: for the things which are seen are temporal; but the things which are not seen are eternal."

The Yali killed the missionaries and ate them. Gruesome, yes, but this was a turning point for other missionaries to come. Within a few years, God's love was reflected in the faces of many Yali.

SCRIPTURES QUOTED: 2 CORINTHIANS 4:17—18

FAITH BELIEVES—THEN SEES

If we are unfaithful, he remains faithful,
for he cannot deny who he is.

2 TIMOTHY 2:13 NLT

A life of unfulfilled promises can leave us jaded. And when we're tempted to live by the motto "I'll believe it when I see it," we need to remember who God is—the Promise Keeper. We can have faith in a faithful God. Scripture says that faith "shows the reality of what we hope for; it is the evidence of things we cannot see." Faith believes first and then sees. Faithfulness is a choice.

"The LORD your God is indeed God. He is the faithful God who keeps his covenant for a thousand generations and lavishes his unfailing love on those who love him and obey his commands." You see, God's faithfulness is perpetual. It doesn't end, take time off, or skip anyone. God wouldn't be God if He were unfaithful. If He said it, then it's a promise kept.

This enormous gap between God's faithfulness and the faithlessness of humanity is yet another example of why your best life can never be here. Your best life can never be now.

Just like grace and mercy, His faithfulness increases our hunger for a better day to come. God gives us glimpses of that day. It's easier to sharpen our focus on that future day when we understand that the attributes of God will replace all the failures we experience in this less-than-best life. God, give us more faith!

SCRIPTURES QUOTED: HEBREWS 11:1; DEUTERONOMY 7:9

KORAH'S REALLY BAD IDEA

Korah son of Izhar. . .became insolent and rose up against Moses.
NUMBERS 16:1−2 NIV

Korah made a poor choice and tried to remove Moses from the position God had appointed him to. And he also enlisted more than two hundred others in his attempted coup.

But these Israelites should have stayed home, because Korah was a faithless man. He thought like a Pharisee and believed he was just as good as and perhaps even holier than Moses. But it wasn't a competition. Moses' brother Aaron reminded Korah that "the whole community is holy, every one of them, and the LORD is with them. Why then do you set yourselves above the LORD's assembly?" Moses responded, "It is against the LORD that you and all your followers have banded together."

The crowd became even bolder, and revolt seemed imminent. But Moses looked at the gathered men and said that if "the earth opens its mouth and swallows them, with everything that belongs to them, and they go down alive into the realm of the dead, then you will know that these men have treated the LORD with contempt." One earth swallow later and everyone knew.

Moses hadn't decided to be the leader of the Israelites. God made that decision. The Lord was faithful even when Korah tried to flex some leadership muscle.

God is faithful even when we are not. Don't assume you know better. Instead, humble yourself, trust God's wisdom, and follow His lead today. He's got this.

SCRIPTURES QUOTED: NUMBERS 16:3, 11, 30

TROUBLE IN TRANSLATION

Let not mercy and truth forsake thee: bind them about thy neck;
write them upon the table of thine heart.

PROVERBS 3:3 KJV

William Tyndale was killed for translating the Bible into English. Church leaders called his translations heresy and passed a death sentence on him. He once said, "I never altered one syllable of God's Word against my conscience, nor would do this day, if all that is in earth, whether it be honor, pleasure, or riches, might be given me."

This Bible translator expressed profound faithfulness to the God who had faithfully given His Word, and he wanted people to read God's promises in their own language. It cost William his life.

But at his death, William knew "this corruptible must put on incorruption, and this mortal must put on immortality." And his worst day ended and a better day arrived. "Know therefore that the LORD thy God, he is God, the faithful God, which keepeth covenant and mercy with them that love him and keep his commandments."

The verses you just read may have been penned by William Tyndale. It's believed that 80 percent of the King James Bible was taken from William's 1500s translation work and used in the King James version in the 1600s.

With every word William translated from Greek to English, he "perceived how that it was impossible to establish the lay people in any truth except the Scripture were plainly laid before their eyes in their mother tongue." He faithfully brought the Bible to people who needed to know what it said.

SCRIPTURES QUOTED: 1 CORINTHIANS 15:53; DEUTERONOMY 7:9

THE GOOD GOD

*Get rid of all bitterness, rage, anger, harsh words, and slander, as well as
all types of evil behavior. Instead, be kind to each other, tenderhearted,
forgiving one another, just as God through Christ has forgiven you.*

EPHESIANS 4:31—32 NLT

It's hard to imagine best-life living in a society defined by bitterness, rage, harsh words, slander, and evil behavior. God asks us to do something that isn't natural to humans. Be kind, tender, and forgiving. It's what God has done for us, so we must do that for others.

God doesn't ask us to pursue our best life. He's always asked us to be in the desperate pursuit of new life. This kind of life offers you the opportunity to "taste and see that the LORD is good."

God is good, but humans are generally selfish. God's goodness is completely unnatural to us—we want what we want and any delay is inexcusable. This kind of thinking motivates unpleasant comments on social media, negative product reviews, and an impatient society.

God has always been different from people. "God loves us, and we have put our trust in his love. God is love, and all who live in love live in God, and God lives in them."

Live for a good God. Allow Him to live in you and make changes. Share His goodness with everyone you meet, and don't slip into selfishness. Resist bitterness, anger, harsh words, and slander. Your better day demands new life today.

SCRIPTURES QUOTED: PSALM 34:8; 1 JOHN 4:16

STEPPING BACK

John replied in the words of Isaiah the prophet, "I am the voice of one
calling in the wilderness, 'Make straight the way for the Lord.'"
JOHN 1:23 NIV

He'd never be rich, and fame still didn't prevent John the Baptist's death.
At the height of John's popularity, Jesus started His ministry. When John
knew he'd met the Messiah, he could only conclude, Jesus "must become
greater; I must become less." Simple as that, John stepped back.

John was given a task by a good God—introduce Jesus, then let Him
do the work. And God asks you to do the same. God had plans for a great
rescue. It required one sacrifice, but many to tell others about what He'd
done. Once you share the news, let God work. Jesus said, "No one can come
to me unless the Father who sent me draws them."

Life isn't all about being noticed. John the Baptist's life suggests we should
seek a life of influence for God's kingdom, but that true fame belongs to
God alone. John Wesley added this perspective, "Do all the good you can,
by all the means you can, in all the ways you can, in all the places you can,
at all the times you can, to all the people you can, as long as ever you can."
Do this and you will influence others on behalf of a famous God.

The plans of our almighty God will always surpass your ideas and exceed
your expectations.

SCRIPTURES QUOTED: JOHN 3:30, 6:44

UPRIGHT AND GOOD

O give thanks unto the LORD; for he is good;
for his mercy endureth for ever.
1 CHRONICLES 16:34 KJV

Edith had gone to hear a man speak about God's lack of goodness and why the Bible couldn't be trusted. At the end of the presentation, a man stepped ahead of her and explained why the speaker's conclusions were wrong. Edith was intrigued by the man, and three years later she married Francis Schaeffer.

The Schaeffers believed that "good and upright is the LORD." They spent the greater part of their lives sharing the goodness of God through the L'Abri organization. They opened their home to travelers who wanted to learn more about the good and upright God.

Before the Schaeffers could ever share God's goodness, they had to commit themselves to this truth: "Thy spirit is good; lead me into the land of uprightness."

Edith was convinced that God was supremely good and that her worst days were not His fault. "Our personal afflictions involve the living God; the only way in which Satan can persecute or afflict God is through attacking the people of God. The only way we can have personal victory in the midst of these flying arrows raining down on us is to call upon the Lord for help. It is His strength, supplied to us in our weakness, that makes victory after victory possible."

SCRIPTURES QUOTED: PSALM 25:8, 143:10

POWER AND GLORY

Yours, O Lord, is the greatness, the power, the glory, the victory, and the majesty. Everything in the heavens and on earth is yours, O Lord, and this is your kingdom. We adore you as the one who is over all things.

1 Chronicles 29:11 nlt

God has a strength we never will. He has power we can't begin to understand. From creation to His movement in every event in human history, God does what we can't. He owns greatness, power, glory, victory, and majesty.

We sacrifice more than we can afford to lose if we keep God at arm's length. And if money becomes our primary goal, we cut our anchor to God's provision. "What do you benefit if you gain the whole world but lose your own soul?"

When pride takes root in our hearts and we refuse His help, He may take a step back to allow us to discover that greatness, power, glory, victory, and majesty were never really ours without Him. Scripture warns: "Don't store up treasures here on earth, where moths eat them and rust destroys them, and where thieves break in and steal. Store your treasures in heaven, where moths and rust cannot destroy, and thieves do not break in and steal."

Material possessions don't last forever, nor can we pack anything we own when our better day welcomes us home. So we simply sacrifice everything we could never keep to experience God's greatness firsthand. His majesty becomes more important than money, His victory means we've overcome, and His glory will bring waves of personal gratitude. The day you witness God's power will be a very good day.

Scriptures quoted: Mark 8:36; Matthew 6:19–20

POWERFUL DISPLAY

The LORD shut him in.
GENESIS 7:16 NIV

The boat God asked Noah to build was mammoth. Animals of all kinds boarded the landlocked vessel to the mocking delight of the gathering crowd outside. And when the people refused to find rescue on board the boat, the Lord shut the door.

God had both the power to save and the power to shut the door. The psalmist described what Noah couldn't see from his vantage point inside the boat: "By the word of the LORD the heavens were made, their starry host by the breath of his mouth."

More than a month passed before the rain ceased its beating on the boat. Eventually the ark rested once again on solid ground, and after the floodwaters receded, Noah's family and the animals left the ark.

Noah and his family could identify with Jeremiah's assessment of God's power: "Ah, Sovereign LORD, you have made the heavens and the earth by your great power and outstretched arm. Nothing is too hard for you."

This boat builder had seen the earth before and after the flood. He heard God's promise and lived to see it fulfilled.

You too have seen the power of God. This power created our world, influences decisions, and prepares a better day. His power offers forever life and helps you recognize that you were rescued. In the presence of God, you'll proclaim His power.

SCRIPTURES QUOTED: PSALM 33:6; JEREMIAH 32:17

HE BRINGS POWER

The LORD shall fight for you, and ye shall hold your peace.
EXODUS 14:14 KJV

Life was difficult for Amy Carmichael—a missionary in India in the early 1900s. She'd overcome many obstacles in order to serve, but the beginnings of her mission work made the impossibilities of her past seem comparatively easy.

Amy witnessed the power of God, though, when she recognized her own weakness. This was, perhaps, no more evident than when she wrote, "To me there is no more tragic sight than the average missionary. . . . We have given so much, yet not the one thing that counts; we aspire so high, and fall so low; we suffer so much, but so seldom with Christ; we have done so much and so little will remain."

Amy addressed child sex trafficking in a significant way. Children were routinely sold into prostitution in India at the time. She rescued dozens of children, but the job was bigger than a missionary from Ireland could manage on her own. Amy learned to "trust ye in the LORD for ever: for in the LORD JEHOVAH is everlasting strength."

God's power was building a kingdom, and His love was making a home. It paid no attention to boundaries, countries, skin color, or language. Every heart can be bent in the direction of God's love, and God's love has the power to change lives. "The kingdom of God is not in word, but in power."

SCRIPTURES QUOTED: ISAIAH 26:4; 1 CORINTHIANS 4:20

COURSE CORRECTION

He is the Rock; his deeds are perfect. Everything he does is just and fair.
He is a faithful God who does no wrong; how just and upright he is!

DEUTERONOMY 32:4 NLT

God is just, but often we allow judgmental attitudes to slip into our mind-set. Judging others isn't the pure pursuit of God's justice, it's merely publicly pointing out the flaws in others.

God gave us His law to show us our error, and He doesn't change His mind about whether we should follow it. God's just nature says the only fair thing for sinners is death—unless someone perfect dies in your place. "The wages of sin is death, but the free gift of God is eternal life through Christ Jesus our Lord."

That's what Jesus did. His grace is an invitation you can accept to your future better day. God's justice leads to an offer of grace: life or death, hope or despair, forgiveness or separation from God. "Everyone who calls on the name of the LORD will be saved."

Often we condemn others without extending to them the same grace and mercy that we have received from the Father. But we can breathe easier knowing that this is not how our Father does things: "God sent his Son into the world not to judge the world, but to save the world through him." God didn't overlook sin, and He corrects our course when we err—but instead of demanding our payment, in His justice and great mercy He saved us from it through Jesus.

SCRIPTURES QUOTED: ROMANS 6:23, 10:13; JOHN 3:17

CORRECTED—NOT CRUSHED

"Teacher, this woman was caught in the act of adultery."
JOHN 8:4 NIV

The mob of religious leaders dragged an adulteress before Jesus and demanded to know if He would stone her as the law commanded. But He disarmed them all when He merely bent and scribbled in the dust as if they weren't trying to back Him into a corner. When they persisted, He said, "Let any one of you who is without sin be the first to throw a stone at her."

Forgiveness doesn't mean no consequences. Jesus simply removed the death penalty for sin with His forgiveness. His grace revealed the rabid judgment of the crowd. They demanded justice but changed their minds when Jesus confronted their hypocrisy.

Jesus defused a mob mentality by introducing them to their own need for forgiveness. And the crowd "began to go away one at a time, the older ones first, until only Jesus was left, with the woman still standing there." She'd expected condemnation and probable death. But instead of death, she encountered new life in Jesus' words: "Neither do I condemn you. Go now and leave your life of sin."

God would rather see a sinner corrected not crushed, restored not ridiculed, and hopeful not humiliated. "He is patient with you, not wanting anyone to perish, but everyone to come to repentance." Take Jesus' counsel: "Go now and leave your life of sin."

SCRIPTURES QUOTED: JOHN 8:7, 9, 11; 2 PETER 3:9

JUDGMENT WITHOUT TRUTH

Above all things have fervent charity among yourselves:
for charity shall cover the multitude of sins.

1 PETER 4:8 KJV

Accusations were easy and arrests were common. More than two hundred names had been mentioned, and justice seemed irrelevant. The witch trials had begun in Salem, Massachusetts.

Some believe this was a time of mass hysteria. The death toll mounted as more and more guilty verdicts were passed. It seemed any small particle of suspicion was justification to declare a new witch in town.

In the spring of 1692, people who claimed to love others chose not to "follow after the things which make for peace, and things wherewith one may edify another." They failed to seek God and as a result chose fear over love— without truth.

History found the Salem witch trials got everything wrong. God's Word would have painted a better picture for those who were seeking judgment above all: "Let not mercy and truth forsake thee: bind them about thy neck; write them upon the table of thine heart: so shalt thou find favour and good understanding in the sight of God and man."

Playing God when passing judgment on others is a dangerous choice. God is big enough to sort out the sins of mankind. He doesn't need help identifying it as every heart is exposed before Him.

God is always just. He knows all. But He is also the source of goodness, mercy, and truth. Speak the truth, but leave the final answer to justice with God.

SCRIPTURES QUOTED: ROMANS 14:19; PROVERBS 3:3—4

NEVER CAUGHT OFF GUARD

Remember the things I have done in the past. For I alone am God! I am God, and there is none like me. Only I can tell you the future before it even happens. Everything I plan will come to pass, for I do whatever I wish.

ISAIAH 46:9—10 NLT

God knows everything, so He's never surprised by a turn of events like we are. When something good happens, it may seem unexpected to us but not to God. When your days are tougher than you'd hoped, God already has a plan to take this bad day and shape it into something good.

He's not caught off guard, doesn't need to read the news, and knows how everything turns out. "The LORD is watching everywhere, keeping his eye on both the evil and the good."

It can be easy to forget that God doesn't wrestle with anxiety. He doesn't wonder what He should do about anything. He simply—yet profoundly—has the world in His hands. This includes the pain you feel, the dreams you dream, and the future that appears as a bold question mark. "God is greater than our feelings, and he knows everything."

When you fully understand that God is aware of your struggle, you might agree to join others in a fraternity of the encouraging: "Be of one mind. Sympathize with each other. Love each other as brothers and sisters. Be tenderhearted." This is how God responds to you in your moments of crisis.

Remember, God can surprise you, but He has never been surprised.

SCRIPTURES QUOTED: PROVERBS 15:3; 1 JOHN 3:20; 1 PETER 3:8

THE OUTCOME

Moses and Aaron went to Pharaoh and said, "This is what the LORD, the God of Israel, says: 'Let my people go, so that they may hold a festival to me in the wilderness.'" Pharaoh said, "Who is the LORD, that I should obey him and let Israel go? I do not know the LORD and I will not let Israel go."

EXODUS 5:1–2 NIV

He was a fearless ruler who believed he could manage any hardship that came along. He'd successfully kept the Israelites, once national guests, as slaves. He made their lives difficult with no plans to let them go.

God knew Pharaoh would be stubborn, so He sent Moses and ten plagues with profound impact. As devastating as each plague was, the doom only made Pharaoh more firm in his resolve to keep God's people from leaving Egypt. This discouraged Moses. "Why, Lord, why have you brought trouble on this people? Is this why you sent me?"

Pharaoh was waging a personal war with God, and Moses wasn't sure God would win. But he didn't need to worry. "I am the LORD, and I will bring you out from under the yoke of the Egyptians. I will free you from being slaves to them, and I will redeem you with an outstretched arm and with mighty acts of judgment. I will take you as my own people, and I will be your God."

Pharaoh thought he could dictate the outcome. And Moses wasn't sure there could be a good outcome. But God wanted everyone to remember that *He* was in control.

SCRIPTURES QUOTED: EXODUS 5:22, 6:6–7

THE STEP OF YES

Who hath directed the Spirit of the LORD, or being his counsellor hath taught him? With whom took he counsel, and who instructed him, and taught him in the path of judgment, and taught him knowledge, and shewed to him the way of understanding?

ISAIAH 40:13–14 KJV

Obeying God leads to His good, perfect, and satisfying life. Brother Andrew was the son of a poor man in the Netherlands. He didn't finish high school and had physical challenges but would ultimately pray, "Lord if You will show me the way, I will follow You." God led. And Andrew followed. This broken man found himself in countries hostile to Christianity. He smuggled Bibles to the spiritually hungry. He brought hope in print. "O the depth of the riches both of the wisdom and knowledge of God! how unsearchable are his judgments, and his ways past finding out."

Andrew prayed, "Whenever, wherever, however you want me, I'll go. . . . I'll begin this very minute. Lord, as I stand up from this place, and as I take my first step forward, will you consider this a step towards complete obedience to you? I'll call it the step of yes."

God wants you to admit He knows it all—recognize this truth and you will embrace awe. "For there is not a word in my tongue, but, lo, O LORD, thou knowest it altogether."

There is a better day coming, and it will always be tied to the presence of a God who isn't surprised that you chose to join Him.

SCRIPTURES QUOTED: ROMANS 11:33; PSALM 139:4

THE LIFE

*"The Father has life in himself, and he has
granted that same life-giving power to his Son."*

JOHN 5:26 NLT

God is wholly self-sufficient and doesn't have needs like we do. Instead He creates and sustains life—like ours. We can't will ourselves to live another day. That's a gift from God.

God meets every need we will ever have. Providing for us isn't just a job to our heavenly Father. He loves us enough to find joy in sustaining us. If God's loving provision is the litmus test for a best day, then every day is our best. And every one of these "best because God loves me" days leads us closer to our better day to come.

God lives forever because He is the fountain of life. He has always owned it. His Son has life-giving power, and when you accept Jesus' rescue plan, He gives eternal life to you. He even said, "I tell you the truth, those who listen to my message and believe in God who sent me have eternal life. They will never be condemned for their sins, but they have already passed from death into life."

The self-sufficiency of God's life is both physical and spiritual. "God is so rich in mercy, and he loved us so much, that even though we were dead because of our sins, he gave us life when he raised Christ from the dead." This is the best life—and you can live it today.

SCRIPTURES QUOTED: JOHN 5:24; EPHESIANS 2:4–5

NEW LIFE FROM
AN OLD CROSS

Three men were fastened to rugged cross timbers to serve out their death sentence. Two were inarguably guilty. But one was without sin. The man in the middle was falsely accused, and while one criminal mocked Him, the other recognized who was hanging beside him: "We are punished justly, for we are getting what our deeds deserve. But this man has done nothing wrong. . . . Jesus, remember me when you come into your kingdom."

He asked the right question of the right man. Imagine how soon the complete weight of his sin was removed—how complete was the blessing of forgiveness. Jesus said words that brought freedom to one crucified: "Truly I tell you, today you will be with me in paradise."

God offers life. Without it there would be no children, no marriage, no one to recognize a gift only God could give. The fact that you can thank God for life is reason enough to applaud the God of the living. He brought life from the cross. He can bring life to the most impossible situations. God has brought *you* life. Live well.

SCRIPTURES QUOTED: LUKE 23:41—42, 43

LIFE AFTER LIFE

*He that walketh righteously, and speaketh uprightly; he that despiseth the
gain of oppressions, that shaketh his hands from holding of bribes,
that stoppeth his ears from hearing of blood, and shutteth
his eyes from seeing evil; he shall dwell on high.*

ISAIAH 33:15—16 KJV

Peter Marshall died when he was just forty-six years old. He lived the
first half of his life in Scotland. When he arrived in the United States, he
attended seminary and learned to become an effective pastor. He spent
time preaching in Georgia and Washington DC before becoming chaplain
to the US Senate in 1947.

Some might call this a rags-to-riches story, but Peter would say, "When we
long for life without difficulties, remind us that oaks grow strong in contrary
winds and diamonds are made under pressure." He learned perseverance.

Peter knew that real life was discovered beyond the confines of human
death, and his better day arrived in 1949. If he could preach one more
sermon, he might have said, "Charge them that are rich in this world, that
they be not highminded, nor trust in uncertain riches, but in the living
God, who giveth us richly all things to enjoy; that they do good, that they
be rich in good works, ready to distribute, willing to communicate; laying
up in store for themselves a good foundation against the time to come, that
they may lay hold on eternal life."

Even death can't end the life God has planned for you. Allow this news
to brighten your outlook.

SCRIPTURES QUOTED: 1 TIMOTHY 6:17—19

GOD'S RECOVERY PLAN

Wisdom from above is first of all pure. It is also peace loving, gentle at all times, and willing to yield to others. It is full of mercy and the fruit of good deeds. It shows no favoritism and is always sincere.

JAMES 3:17 NLT

God is wise, and He is the source of all true wisdom.

If your wisdom isn't from God, then expect your decisions to lead you into some problems. Perfectly harmonious living doesn't exist here on earth because if our own sins aren't stealing our peace, then someone else's certainly will. Not everyone who follows Jesus also follows His wisdom.

Take ownership of every decision, and discover that decision-making on your own often results in failure. "No one can ever boast in the presence of God. God has united you with Christ Jesus. For our benefit God made him to be wisdom itself. Christ made us right with God; he made us pure and holy, and he freed us from sin."

Jesus is wisdom personified. His word offers a warning for those who would seek wisdom elsewhere, "Don't let anyone capture you with empty philosophies and high-sounding nonsense that come from human thinking and from the spiritual powers of this world, rather than from Christ."

Missionary David Brainerd understood how much humans could mess things up: "The all-seeing eye of God beheld our deplorable state; infinite pity touched the heart of the Father of mercies; and infinite wisdom laid the plan of our recovery." Jesus is your wisdom recovery plan.

SCRIPTURES QUOTED: 1 CORINTHIANS 1:29–30; COLOSSIANS 2:8

CHOOSE YOUR GIFT WISELY

God gave Solomon wisdom and very great insight, and a breadth of understanding as measureless as the sand on the seashore. . . . He was wiser than anyone else.

1 KINGS 4:29, 31 NIV

God gave young King Solomon something far better than an unlimited credit card, handmade gift, or an expensive car. He told the new king, "Ask for whatever you want me to give you." Had any gift like this been given before? Solomon replied, "Give me wisdom and knowledge, that I may lead this people, for who is able to govern this great people of yours?"

God thought this was a great choice: "Wisdom and knowledge will be given you. And I will also give you wealth, possessions and honor, such as no king who was before you ever had and none after you will have."

Watchman Nee understood this: "If whatever men know comes through their brain without the Holy Spirit regenerating their spirit, then their knowledge will help them not one whit. If their belief rests in man's wisdom and not in God's power, they are merely excited in their soul."

God's wisdom directs decisions, futures, and careers. It's always the best choice. All you have to do is ask for it. "If any of you lacks wisdom, you should ask God, who gives generously to all without finding fault, and it will be given to you."

There's no knowledge God hasn't already mastered, and He can teach you. Just *ask*. Make this a premium gift request. God executed a divine rescue plan and offers the wisdom to really live a new life.

SCRIPTURES QUOTED: 2 CHRONICLES 1:7, 10, 12; JAMES 1:5

IT STARTED WITH WISDOM

Be ye not unwise, but understanding what the will of the Lord is.
EPHESIANS 5:17 KJV

Matthew Henry may not be as well known as other Christians who impacted their world for God, but his passion began with learning Latin and Greek when he was nine years old. By learning from some of the original texts of the Bible, Matthew began a lifelong effort to help others understand the Bible. He wrote commentaries on both the Old and New Testaments before he passed away in 1714.

He sought wisdom, and God is good at answering that kind of prayer. "Let the word of Christ dwell in you richly in all wisdom; teaching and admonishing one another in psalms and hymns and spiritual songs, singing with grace in your hearts to the Lord."

Many preachers have used Matthew Henry's commentaries. One of his most famous observations was about Adam and Eve: "The woman was made of a rib out of the side of Adam; not made out of his head to rule over him, nor out of his feet to be trampled upon by him, but out of his side to be equal with him, under his arm to be protected, and near his heart to be beloved."

Real learning always stems from wisdom. "Wisdom is the principal thing; therefore get wisdom: and with all thy getting get understanding." Wisdom is truth—understanding is knowing what to do with the truth.

SCRIPTURES QUOTED: COLOSSIANS 3:16; PROVERBS 4:7

GOD PLACES

I can never escape from your Spirit! I can never get away from your presence!
If I go up to heaven, you are there; if I go down to the grave, you are there.
If I ride the wings of the morning, if I dwell by the farthest oceans,
even there your hand will guide me, and your strength will support me.

PSALM 139:7–10 NLT

Challenge God to a race and you'll lose every time—because no place exists where God is not. You can't beat Him there, and He stays after you leave.

God walks with you in the sunlight and in the quiet place where sin gives birth. He knows what seems unknowable and goes where no one has been. And all of this is less about being invasive and more about being near you on days that are less than your best.

God wants to be sure you understand this truth. He asks, "Can anyone hide from me in a secret place? Am I not everywhere in all the heavens and earth?" You can't hide from God because He's everywhere. And just in case you need another example of God's inescapable presence: "Heaven is my throne, and the earth is my footstool."

The best life you can have here is linked to the closeness of a good God. He doesn't promise perfect days but rather a perfect closeness when trouble comes.

SCRIPTURES QUOTED: JEREMIAH 23:24; ISAIAH 66:1

GOD STAYED

*[Barnabas] was a good man, full of the Holy Spirit and faith,
and a great number of people were brought to the Lord.*
ACTS 11:24 NIV

His real name was Joseph, but most people called him Barnabas, meaning "Son of Encouragement." He was certainly an encouragement to the apostle Paul, originally called Saul. The two were regular partners on mission trips designed to share God's good news. They were a dynamic duo that served the *everywhere* God.

Barnabas had to see clearly that God was everywhere. No matter where he went, hearts were prepared before the missionaries arrived. "Sergius Paulus. . .sent for Barnabas and Saul because he wanted to hear the word of God." Then "the people invited them to speak further."

God went before Barnabas and Paul, preparing people to hear the message they had always needed to hear. God walked with the missionaries, arranged everything before they arrived, and stayed behind to help those who listened. Because He's God, He could do all of this simultaneously.

Even after Paul and Barnabas had moved on, God was still working in people's lives. Paul said, "Let us go back and visit the believers in all the towns where we preached the word of the Lord and see how they are doing."

When they returned to the people they'd met, they saw believers who had grown in their faith—because even after the ministers left, God stayed.

SCRIPTURES QUOTED: ACTS 13:7, 42; 15:36

THE WALL

Will God indeed dwell on the earth? behold,
the heaven and heaven of heavens cannot contain thee.

1 KINGS 8:27 KJV

Adoniram Judson was smarter than most. He could read at three and studied advanced subjects before ten. Sometimes really smart people are less willing to believe in God. That described Adoniram.

His father was a preacher, and his mother pleaded with him to follow Jesus, but the intellectual words of a deist caused Adoniram to walk away from the always-present God and deny His existence. But the truth remained in the words of the Bible: "As truly as I live, all the earth shall be filled with the glory of the LORD."

Ironically, the man who persuaded Adoniram to distance himself from God was instrumental in bringing him face-to-face with his need for God. Adoniram was sleeping in a small inn when he heard the moans of someone nearing death. The sad sounds made him think about life after death, and he considered the words of his parents—and God. The dying man was the same one who had convinced Adoniram to turn his back on God.

This young deist then made a choice to honor the God of the prophet Isaiah's great vision, where angels cried, "Holy, holy, holy, is the LORD of hosts: the whole earth is full of his glory."

Once Adoniram surrendered to the everywhere God, he began a journey that changed the nation of Burma. He became a missionary and brought the Gospel to a nation waiting to hear.

You too can walk with God.

SCRIPTURES QUOTED: NUMBERS 14:21; ISAIAH 6:3

ROADBLOCK REGRET

"Repent of your sins and turn to God, so that your sins may be wiped away."
ACTS 3:19 NLT

Sadly, our *better day to come* might have to wait until heaven because of personal regret. Our own poor decisions and the resulting sorrow may put up roadblocks to experiencing good days.

The good news is you can allow God to remove these roadblocks through forgiveness. Forgiveness leans in to God's strength and declares victory. "For the kind of sorrow God wants us to experience leads us away from sin and results in salvation. There's no regret for that kind of sorrow. But worldly sorrow, which lacks repentance, results in spiritual death."

The sorrow that moves you to God's side has His stamp of approval. Sorrow that doesn't lead away from sin is not only meaningless emotion, but it keeps you separated from the God who gives life—not a great place to exist.

People who live in the land of regret torture themselves with bad memories and self-condemnation. They find no way to redeem those bad decisions, just a perpetual acceptance of personal failure. Regret is useful in identifying sin, but once we're forgiven—because we repent or turn away from sin—then there is no longer a reason to make regret our companion. "[God] has removed our sins as far from us as the east is from the west."

You will have regrets, but you can release them to the God who forgives. Let them go.

SCRIPTURES QUOTED: 2 CORINTHIANS 7:10; PSALM 103:12

I have seen all the works that are done under the sun;
and, behold, all is vanity and vexation of spirit.
ECCLESIASTES 1:14 KJV

King Solomon had everything, but it wasn't enough. The book of Ecclesiastes has a deep vein of regret running through it.

How is it possible for a king who had it all to dine on a buffet of regret, apathy, indifference, and cynicism? This emotional diet made it hard for King Solomon to find a reason to worship the Gift Giver.

Zephaniah described a moment when many people expressed similar indifference: "The LORD will not do good, neither will he do evil." They were essentially saying that God couldn't hurt them, but neither could He help them. This was more than apathy. It was an indication that they felt God could not be trusted because He wasn't near enough to do anything. Maybe He didn't even exist.

Believing that God is powerless can have us thinking our best life is now—that there isn't anything better to look forward to and that God has very little to do with helping anyone now or in the future.

Solomon had everything he wanted but forgot the One who met needs. When he spent time indulging His wants, he misplaced his joy. This led Solomon to say, "What profit hath a man of all his labour which he taketh under the sun?"

Choose to accept forgiveness, not Solomon's regret buffet.

SCRIPTURES QUOTED: ZEPHANIAH 1:12; ECCLESIASTES 1:3

GOING HIS WAY

Not forsaking the assembling of ourselves together, as the manner of some is; but exhorting one another: and so much the more, as ye see the day approaching.

HEBREWS 10:25 KJV

Before Susannah became the wife of Charles Spurgeon, she found her faith had run cold. Suzannah began her journey with Jesus but had no idea how to grow. Like a glowing ember removed from a flame, her brightness dimmed. She knew she wanted to follow God—she just didn't know how to get from where she was to where she needed to be.

She may have thought this time was wasted, but she would go on to be a powerful witness for Jesus. She planted a church, encouraged her husband in his ministry, and started a ministry to pastors and families who struggled. She was an author who wrote eloquently about faith. But something had to happen first. She needed direction and she found it: "Shew me thy ways, O LORD; teach me thy paths. Lead me in thy truth, and teach me: for thou art the God of my salvation; on thee do I wait all the day."

It's discouraging to know that you should follow God but have no idea how. But it's hard to worship God *and* be apathetic.

Following God can easily start with this prayer: "Teach me to do thy will; for thou art my God: thy spirit is good; lead me into the land of uprightness."

Follow God and ask for His help. He will lead you.

SCRIPTURES QUOTED: PSALM 25:4–5, 143:10

SECURE

Do not love this world nor the things it offers you, for when you love the world, you do not have the love of the Father in you.

1 JOHN 2:15 NLT

Everyone has insecurities. Maybe you don't know where you fit in, you fear rejection if people get to know you, or you worry about being judged by others. We all try to mask our insecurity in different ways—some lash out and others hide in the background.

But know this: God knows you, loves you, and wants to call you His child. Isn't it easier to find security with Someone who makes you secure? "He lifted me out of the pit of despair, out of the mud and the mire. He set my feet on solid ground and steadied me as I walked along."

He's not condemning each step you take. He knows you'll fail, but He reaches down where you are and pulls you up and out of the junk that's stuck to you like glue. Get acquainted with solid ground and accept His steady leadership.

It's hard to have your best day when you struggle with insecurity. It's equally as difficult when you're surrounded with people who are also insecure (and that's everyone). The only secure thing you can hang on to is God. Search Him out. "Those who know your name trust in you, for you, O LORD, do not abandon those who search for you."

SCRIPTURES QUOTED: PSALM 40:2, 9:10

THE INSECURE WARRIOR

When the angel of the LORD appeared to Gideon, he said,
"The LORD is with you, mighty warrior."
JUDGES 6:12 NIV

Gideon had a close encounter with one of God's messenger angels. He heard the words, "The LORD is with you," and the term "mighty warrior" applied to him, but the angel must have been confused. Gideon had been hiding from the Midianites to keep them from stealing his wheat. What kind of warrior does that?

But God wanted to use Gideon to conquer the enemy. The Lord said, "Go in the strength you have and save Israel out of Midian's hand. Am I not sending you?"

Gideon was insecure. He didn't think of himself as strong, and he had no idea how to save the people of Israel. In his trepidation he asked, "Pardon me, my lord, but how can I save Israel? My clan is the weakest in Manasseh, and I am the least in my family." God wanted to use him, and Gideon threw himself a pity party. He claimed to be the least important person from the weakest clan.

When God finally got Gideon ready for battle, He stretched his security even further. God made him send home nearly thirty-two thousand soldiers who came out to fight the Midianites. Only three hundred soldiers remained. God led Gideon to a very unique and total victory. Stop—this is important: God loves insecure people. He uses insecure people. He makes insecure people. . .secure.

Your day becomes better when you're certain that the God who fashioned you can also take care of you. He can make you secure.

SCRIPTURES QUOTED: JUDGES 6:14, 15

WHO ARE YOU?

Peace I leave with you, my peace I give unto you: not as the world giveth,
give I unto you. Let not your heart be troubled, neither let it be afraid.
JOHN 14:27 KJV

Body shaming is a way for people to project their insecurity onto others. They criticize others for being too tall or too short, weighing less than some or more than most, being obsessed about appearance or not seeming to care. Mandisa felt shame in front of a national audience.

She'd been accepted to a nationally televised singing competition, and she'd done very well. She found herself in the top ten. She'd also heard one judge make continued negative comments about her looks. She was hurt and insecure. Even when she made healthy lifestyle changes, she still couldn't block out the criticism.

Maybe you could use a shot of good news: "There is therefore now no condemnation to them which are in Christ Jesus, who walk not after the flesh, but after the Spirit."

Follow God and discover a distinct lack of condemnation. Who wouldn't love that? It doesn't matter what you look like, what skills you possess, or who your parents are. That's security and freedom. That's what gives you the heart of an overcomer. "For whatsoever is born of God overcometh the world: and this is the victory that overcometh the world, even our faith. Who is he that overcometh the world, but he that believeth that Jesus is the Son of God?"

SCRIPTURES QUOTED: ROMANS 8:1; 1 JOHN 5:4–5

DECLARED NOT GUILTY

Keeping our eyes on Jesus, the champion who initiates and perfects our faith. Because of the joy awaiting him, he endured the cross, disregarding its shame. Now he is seated in the place of honor beside God's throne.

HEBREWS 12:2 NLT

Have you ever felt guilty. . .because you *were* guilty? Have you felt shame because you did something shameful or judged because you did something worth judging?

Answer yes to any of these questions and join the 100 percent of people who recognize guilt. We've all experienced the debilitating feelings that come with being guilty.

Guilty people never live their best life. Instead it feels as if they've lost the chance to be anything better than their worst mistake. But we've got an Advocate. Someone's in your corner. And it's not all bad—guilt can motivate us to seek forgiveness. "But if anyone does sin, we have an advocate who pleads our case before the Father. He is Jesus Christ, the one who is truly righteous."

This isn't an isolated bit of good news for guilty people. "There is one God and one Mediator who can reconcile God and humanity—the man Christ Jesus."

Guilt is easy to accept and hard to release. When God accepted Jesus' sacrifice, you were reconciled to God. And when you accept forgiveness, you *are* forgiven. When you're declared "Not guilty," you're not guilty. You were once guilty and on your way to an eternity separated from God, but God made it possible for you to prepare for your best day ever.

SCRIPTURES QUOTED: 1 JOHN 2:1; 1 TIMOTHY 2:5

GUILT AND THE STRONG MAN

Blessed is the one whose transgressions are forgiven, whose sins are covered.
Blessed is the one whose sin the LORD does not count against them.

PSALM 32:1–2 NIV

Samson was set apart as a Nazarite. His life was to be in service to God. As long as he didn't cut his hair, he possessed a superhero-like strength. This would have been enough for most, but it was common to the man who'd never known physical weakness.

Guilt trailed the strongman—fits of anger and violence, adultery, and being influenced by those who were against God. For a man who was supposed to be set apart *for* God, it seemed Samson was determined to be set *against* God.

Delilah was the second Philistine woman Samson fell in love with. She worked overtime to discover the secret to his strength, and he lied to her repeatedly. But he eventually confessed, "No razor has ever been used on my head because I have been a Nazirite dedicated to God from my mother's womb. If my head were shaved, my strength would leave me, and I would become as weak as any other man."

Later, Samson had plenty of time to consider his guilt. . .that was after Delilah had his head shaved while he slept and the Philistines took his eyes. Samson went from judge in Israel to "grinding grain in the prison." His power didn't come from his long hair. Samson was strong because he obeyed the God who made him strong. Guilt separates you from God, but forgiveness brings you back to His side.

SCRIPTURES QUOTED: JUDGES 16:17, 21

GUILT REPLACEMENT

*Let us draw near with a true heart in full assurance of faith, having our hearts
sprinkled from an evil conscience, and our bodies washed with pure water.*

HEBREWS 10:22 KJV

He was glad his family could take an ocean voyage to England. They needed
the time away, but he was a busy lawyer and stayed behind. Work took Horatio Spafford's mind off his losses. His son had died just two years before.
Then he invested in Chicago real estate, but the Great Chicago Fire of 1871
destroyed most of his investments. So he worked.

Then came an earth-shattering telegram of two words: SAVED ALONE.
Suddenly, it seemed foolish to allow work to become so important. His
four daughters died in an ocean collision, and his wife was the only family
member to survive. On the way to be with her, Horatio watched the relentless
waves, then he wrote, "When peace, like a river, attendeth my way, when
sorrows like sea billows roll; whatever my lot, Thou hast taught me to say,
it is well, it is well with my soul."

He questioned whether he could have saved his daughters and why work
was so important. What's the use of gaining more things when he could have
spent time with family? But through Christ, his guilt was replaced by peace,
his sorrow assuaged with assurance.

God never wants guilt to be your final response. Guilt should always lead
to repentance. Repentance should always lead to forgiveness. And forgiveness leads to restored righteousness before a good God. "If we confess our
sins, he is faithful and just to forgive us our sins, and to cleanse us from
all unrighteousness."

SCRIPTURE QUOTED: 1 JOHN 1:9

IMPERFECTIONS

*I don't mean to say that I have already achieved these things or that
I have already reached perfection. But I press on to possess that
perfection for which Christ Jesus first possessed me.*

PHILIPPIANS 3:12 NLT

Just as staring at your reflection reveals your flaws, looking into the mirror of
God's Word lays bare the pieces of us that don't resemble the God we follow.

Physical and spiritual imperfections are to be expected. But we're more
than a walking mass of flaws. "Thank you for making me so wonderfully
complex! Your workmanship is marvelous—how well I know it."

God doesn't see what you see. He was very clear there's a significant
difference in His outlook. "The LORD doesn't see things the way you see
them. People judge by outward appearance, but the LORD looks at the heart."

God has a different body waiting for you on that better day to come. It
won't be like your current body—it'll be perfect and last forever.

If we focus on our undesirable features, the enemy can convince us that
God didn't make us wonderfully, that He made a mistake. You've seen the
magazine covers and watched the movies. It seems there are perfect people
who must enjoy a perfect life while you must endure imperfection. It doesn't
seem fair. But what you see isn't reality. Everyone has flaws. Everyone has
something they wish was different. Remember, God doesn't see the flaws—
He's paying too much attention to your heart. What's He discovering today?

SCRIPTURES QUOTED: PSALM 139:14; 1 SAMUEL 16:7

PERFECT KINDNESS

Mephibosheth bowed down and said, "What is your servant,
that you should notice a dead dog like me?"

2 SAMUEL 9:8 NIV

David and Jonathan had been the best of friends. Jonathan was willing to give up his right to be king so David could take the throne. Then Jonathan died and David became king.

Mephibosheth was Jonathan's son who was "lame in both feet." He had to have someone help him wherever he went. This young man even referred to himself as a dead dog. His imperfections were frustrating to him, and he could likely remember the day he learned that his grandfather, King Saul, and his father had been killed—the same day the accident happened. He had been dropped as a five-year-old, permanently injuring his feet.

But King David found him and welcomed him to eat at his table. Mephibosheth and his family were well taken care of by the king who didn't look at the young man's imperfections but on the friendship he'd had with Jonathan.

This is a picture of the way God deals with your imperfections. For the sake of His Son, Jesus, He is kind. God honors His Son, and because of that love, imperfections become perfect in His sight. "Indeed, there is no one on earth who is righteous, no one who does what is right and never sins." Jesus is perfect, and *that's* what God sees in you when you're forgiven. And that makes for a very good day.

SCRIPTURES QUOTED: 2 SAMUEL 9:13; ECCLESIASTES 7:20

AMAZED

*Now we exhort you, brethren, warn them that are unruly, comfort the
feebleminded, support the weak, be patient toward all men.*

1 THESSALONIANS 5:14 KJV

Nick Vujicic was born without arms or legs—a condition known as phocome-
lia. He was an imperfect baby, and his parents struggled to accept their son.
Their initial reaction proves that every human is subject to disappointment
and hurt. Like most kids, Nick was intent on learning to do everything he
could for himself, but he learned there were things he could not do without
help. Learning to lean on our heavenly Father is also important to understanding the Christian walk.

Today Nick is married, the father of four children, and an international
speaker. His appearance makes people curious, but his story breaks down the
walls for those who feel awkward about his imperfections. When his better
day comes, Nick will discover God's perfection, but he'll also remember
God's grace. He'll turn new hands and look at new fingers. He'll walk. He'll
clap. He may even laugh in amazement. For today, Nick is only too aware
that he's actually not so different from others. They may have arms, legs,
hands, and feet, but they also live with personal struggle.

No one's immune to imperfections. Every struggle is real and very
personal. Lean on God in prayer today: "Thou, which hast shewed me great
and sore troubles, shalt. . .bring me up again from the depths of the earth.
Thou shalt. . .comfort me on every side."

SCRIPTURES QUOTED: PSALM 71:20–21

PRESSED. PERPLEXED.
HUNTED. KNOCKED DOWN.

We are pressed on every side by troubles, but we are not crushed.
We are perplexed, but not driven to despair. We are hunted down,
but never abandoned by God. We get knocked down,
but we are not destroyed.

2 Corinthians 4:8–9 NLT

Charles Spurgeon once wrote, "The Lord gets his best soldiers out of the highlands of affliction." Maybe you're surveying your life's damage from Affliction Ridge. But the fact that you can look back means you survived. Squeezed but never crushed, perplexed but not in despair, and sometimes knocked down but never destroyed—you are a child of God, and He protects His family.

God's Word says, "The righteous person faces many troubles, but the Lord comes to the rescue each time." Pray on the bad days: "Turn to me and have mercy, for I am alone and in deep distress. My problems go from bad to worse. Oh, save me from them all! Feel my pain and see my trouble."

The Bible proves there is no truth to the often-quoted but unbiblical phrase "God helps those who help themselves." You will go through struggles. You will be afflicted. And suffering is guaranteed. But you're never abandoned by God. *Never.*

Author and preacher John Bunyan provides a great reminder of this never-abandoned truth: "In times of affliction we commonly meet with the sweetest experiences of the love of God."

There's victory for the afflicted, hope for the perplexed, and help for the knocked down. You've been all three. This is good news delivered.

Scriptures quoted: Psalm 34:19. 25:16–18

THE MERCY CALL

As [Jesus] was going into a village, ten men who had leprosy met him.
They stood at a distance and called out in a loud voice,
"Jesus, Master, have pity on us!"

LUKE 17:12–13 NIV

It wasn't a late-night zombie movie, but it was just as scary for those who saw the men with leprosy walking their way calling out, "Unclean." No one was exactly sure how the disease spread, but those with the wasting skin had to live outside town with others suffering from the same affliction. Fear followed the leper. People changed direction when they showed up. Conversations were rarely civil.

Then came ten men with various stages of leprosy. They saw Jesus and were quick to ask for help. They'd heard people talk about Jesus. This could be their best chance for regaining a normal life. They all wanted to go home. Could Jesus do the impossible and heal them?

After Jesus healed them, these men were no longer afflicted with leprosy, but instead forgetfulness. Only "one of them, when he saw he was healed, came back, praising God in a loud voice. He threw himself at Jesus' feet and thanked him—and he was a Samaritan."

Only one of the afflicted thought enough of the life-changing gift to show gratitude. Only one praised God even though he was not an Israelite. It must have been easy for Jesus to say, "Rise and go; your faith has made you well."

SCRIPTURES QUOTED: LUKE 17:15–16, 19

THIS WAS AFFLICTION

What shall we then say to these things?
If God be for us, who can be against us?
ROMANS 8:31 KJV

Martin and Gracia Burnham were married for eighteen years, most of which they spent as missionaries. They celebrated their anniversary by booking a stay at the Dos Palmas Resort in the Philippines. But in the spring of 2001, the couple was captured by the militant group Abu Sayyaf. And they weren't the only ones.

Many of those kidnapped were later released. But after a year, Martin and Gracia were still in captivity with three kids praying that their parents would be released. This was affliction and a temptation to despair. This was hope deferred.

They were moved from one place to the next for more than a year. The couple lost weight, strength, and endurance. They were disconnected from any human encouragement, but God was with them in every new place they were forced to go. "He hath not despised nor abhorred the affliction of the afflicted; neither hath he hid his face from him; but when he cried unto him, he heard."

Martin was welcomed to his better day in heaven when Gracia was freed midyear 2002. Gracia received bullet wounds, but both she and Martin experienced their own freedom. Now she will wait to see Martin again, but the affliction led Gracia only to spend more time in the presence of the same God who encourages you to "be strong and of a good courage; be not afraid, neither be thou dismayed: for the Lord thy God is with thee whithersoever thou goest."

SCRIPTURES QUOTED: PSALM 22:24; JOSHUA 1:9

NO COMPARISON

*Oh, don't worry; we wouldn't dare say that we are as wonderful as
these other men who tell you how important they are! But they are
only comparing themselves with each other, using themselves
as the standard of measurement. How ignorant!*

2 Corinthians 10:12 NLT

If you compare yourself to another person, one of you will always seem to
come out on top. And whatever the comparison outcome, you will either
feel superior or crushed. You'll proclaim your excellence or lament your
mediocrity. But God says this kind of comparison is "ignorant." Why? The
only one God ever compares you to is Jesus—and He's always the best.

If you're curious why God compares you to perfection, it's not to say, "Hey,
My Son is best," although He is. God compares you to His Son because the
only thing that can save you is Jesus' perfection. God accepts that perfection
on your behalf. He means to move you from condemned to rescued. It's
designed to keep you from boasting.

Comparing yourself to Jesus gives you a greater appreciation for what
God has done for you. "Examine yourselves to see if your faith is genuine.
Test yourselves. Surely you know that Jesus Christ is among you; if not, you
have failed the test of genuine faith."

Think about this: "What do you have that God hasn't given you? And if
everything you have is from God, why boast as though it were not a gift?"
Compare yourself to Jesus. And because He wins, so do you. Embrace His gift.

Scriptures quoted: 2 Corinthians 13:5; 1 Corinthians 4:7

COMPARING SIBLINGS

The first to come out was red, and his whole body was
like a hairy garment; so they named him Esau.

GENESIS 25:25 NIV

Jacob and Esau, twin brothers who were compared from birth. Their dad, Issac, loved Esau, while mom was much fonder of Jacob. These brothers did not look the same. Esau was hairy and red while Jacob was smooth skinned.

Siblings have heard parents say things like, "Why can't you be more like your brother?" But this question never stems from compassion. The Bible even shares one of these comparisons between the twins: "The boys grew up, and Esau became a skillful hunter, a man of the open country, while Jacob was content to stay at home among the tents."

Comparison did not lead to best-life living for either brother. Esau felt as if Jacob had tricked him one too many times and wanted to kill his brother. Esau said, "Isn't he rightly named Jacob? This is the second time he has taken advantage of me: He took my birthright, and now he's taken my blessing!" Neither brother was perfect, and they knew how to push each other's buttons.

This rift between siblings meant the brothers stayed away from each other for more than two decades. What might their lives have been like if they'd lived lives without comparison? What would your life be like without comparison? After all, comparing yourself to others will never make you more like God.

Using others as your standard doesn't generally bring out mercy and compassion. Instead, we're much more prone to boast or criticize when comparisons are made. And usually they hurt.

SCRIPTURES QUOTED: GENESIS 25:27, 27:36

NO EGO

The Lord will perfect that which concerneth me.
PSALM 138:8 KJV

Luis Palau was doing good work for Billy Graham. He didn't seem to have a reason to try something new. Yet he had the desire to follow God's big adventure for him. So he stepped out when he was called.

Billy understood God was working on Luis and provided financial help to allow him to move forward with his dream. No comparisons. No egos. No tension. "For I say. . .to every man that is among you, not to think of himself more highly than he ought to think; but to think soberly."

Luis had a heart for young people, and that difference set him apart from Billy. He was no better or worse, just different. He wasn't designed to be an exact copy of Billy Graham. He didn't have to focus on the same ministry purpose, and he didn't have to act like Billy because he wasn't Billy.

God made their dreams different. He took the purpose of two men and added His power. You can *enhance* the work God has given to someone else and never *compare* what they're doing with what you have done. Here's the reason: "We have many members in one body, and all members have not the same office: So we, being many, are one body in Christ, and every one members one of another." Everyone has a unique purpose and position in God's kingdom. Let's stop comparing and start working together.

SCRIPTURES QUOTED: ROMANS 12:3, 4–5

DIVISIVE

And now I make one more appeal, my dear brothers and sisters.
Watch out for people who cause divisions and upset people's faith by teaching
things contrary to what you have been taught. Stay away from them.

ROMANS 16:17 NLT

People who cause divisions may not be your enemy, but they make life hard. Or maybe you've been the one driving in the wedge a time or two. God wants you to know that "such people are not serving Christ our Lord; they are serving their own personal interests."

You don't want that to be said about you, and frankly it's tough to call someone out on their own fits of division. Many divisions grow out of self-focused thought patterns: "These people are grumblers and complainers, living only to satisfy their desires. They brag loudly about themselves."

Sound familiar? Even if you're having the best day you've had in a long time, it can be shaken like a soda can by whiners. These kinds of people have little problem fracturing relationships. . .it even seems as if they enjoy it.

There's a reason God calls for unity among His people. Some of it has to do with the increasingly negative consequences of division. Call it poking the bear, pressing buttons, or even getting under someone's skin if you like, but God calls it division—and it's wrong. It doesn't line up with His command to love.

Remember that division honors no one but self. Unity honors God and others.

SCRIPTURES QUOTED: ROMANS 16:18; JUDE 16

DIVIDE AND CONFUSE

[Judas asked,] "Why wasn't this perfume sold and the money given to the poor? It was worth a year's wages."

JOHN 12:5 NIV

Mary had just anointed Jesus' feet with very expensive perfume. Most saw the gesture as a lavish honor for their beloved teacher. But Judas, in his greed, hammered a wedge into the otherwise praiseworthy expression. The Bible is clear that this disciple didn't admire the gesture, but he did covet the value of the gift. As the resident financial advisor, Judas was the "keeper of the money bag," who just happened to be skimming off the top for personal use.

Judas developed a pattern of divide and confuse. He conspired with religious leaders to arrest Jesus and lied to Jesus about his willingness to betray. He used a kiss, the sign of friendship, to help soldiers identify Jesus. And when it was clear he had been successful, Judas did get some money for his efforts—but it wasn't as satisfying as he expected. "When Judas, who had betrayed him, saw that Jesus was condemned, he was seized with remorse and returned the thirty pieces of silver to the chief priests and the elders."

Judas was wrong but didn't ask for forgiveness. He saw miracles but didn't seek one. He knew the truth but sought to dilute it. Don't get caught on the side of division. It may seem strategic, but it doesn't serve the best interest of others—or the heart of God.

SCRIPTURES QUOTED: JOHN 12:6; MATTHEW 27:3

TOGETHER IN HARMONY

*Behold, how good and how pleasant it is
for brethren to dwell together in unity!*
PSALM 133:1 KJV

Very few people encourage unity like a worship leader, at least for a few minutes. And music was the pinnacle of importance to Ira Sanky in the late 1800s.

Dwight Moody would ask Ira to lead music in his crusades. Eventually, Ira did join Dwight and transformed the way music was used in a worship service. Music was revolutionary to Ira, and he brought the revolution to those who should "with one mind and one mouth glorify God, even the Father of our Lord Jesus Christ."

Once Dwight and Ira visited a gypsy camp outside London. Ira prayed with a fifteen-year-old boy and told him one day he would become a preacher. Fifteen years later, this same boy, then known as Gipsy Smith, said, "Save a boy, and you save a multiplication table."

One man seeking unity among believers led one boy to multiply blessings to many. Ira didn't leave him out. The love of God opened the door to opportunity. "Be of the same mind one toward another. Mind not high things, but condescend to men of low estate. Be not wise in your own conceits."

God can take what you do and unify people in faith. It may mean resisting unkind words. It may mean giving a little more of your time than you planned. And it will absolutely mean more than you expect.

SCRIPTURES QUOTED: ROMANS 15:6, 12:16

FAITH'S FAMILY REUNION

By faith we understand that the universe was formed at God's command.
HEBREWS 11:3 NIV

Hebrews 11 is forty verses of hall of fame material—an award show of the faithful with red carpet treatment. This chapter names the heroes one by one: Abel, Enoch, Noah, Abraham, Sarah, Jacob, Joseph, and the list goes on. It's a celebration of those who walked out their faith, a list of the imperfect but believing, and an encouragement to us.

This chapter celebrates the best life possible, when joy is recognized and God's love is on display. "This is what the ancients were commended for." They knew their best life on earth could only happen when they trusted that God knew what He was doing. It wasn't found in their demanding a new house, wheels, or job. God had a good plan all along, and these heroes showed a remarkable trust in following the Leader.

The Bible suggests that God "planned something better for us so that only together with us would they be made perfect." These heroes of the faith are waiting for your ultimate better day, for a future family gathering with you.

They experienced the best life possible, but it was only a dim reflection of the future day when heaven is home and God is your neighbor.

SCRIPTURES QUOTED: HEBREWS 11:2, 40

*O God, you are my God; I earnestly search for you. My soul thirsts
for you; my whole body longs for you in this parched
and weary land where there is no water.*

PSALM 63:1 NLT

Best-life living is hard to find in a parched and weary place. This personal wasteland serves as a reminder of how bleak things are without God. Sometimes it's hard to find a reason to keep trying when injustice is the new norm. But God wants more for your life than just a survival existence.

Don't be deceived into believing that God is hidden from you. He's near and He cares. He's compassionate toward your struggles. He refreshes and restores your flagging resolve. He is the forever norm, and nothing can stand against Him.

The best life possible in the here and now includes obedience to the God who has answers. Jesus made this point when He said, "All who love me will do what I say. My Father will love them, and we will come and make our home with each of them."

Does that sound like a God who is standoffish? Does it remind you of someone unwilling to help? "Seek the LORD while you can find him. Call on him now while he is near. Let the wicked change their ways and banish the very thought of doing wrong. Let them turn to the LORD that he may have mercy on them. Yes, turn to our God, for he will forgive generously."

Seek. Find. Follow.

SCRIPTURES QUOTED: JOHN 14:23; ISAIAH 55:6–7

DON'T STOP SEEKING

The angel said to him: "Do not be afraid, Zechariah; your prayer has been heard. Your wife Elizabeth will bear you a son, and you are to call him John."
LUKE 1:13 NIV

Zechariah sought the God of his fathers for most of his life. He was a priest and, if asked, would have said God was important and trustworthy. But "they were childless because Elizabeth was not able to conceive, and they were both very old." Following God was Zechariah's best life, but he forfeited the best in favor of disbelief.

After all, people their age didn't have children, and the couple had come to terms with the lack of a child. When an angel promised something that sounded a lot like the stories Zechariah had read about Abraham, the priest's hesitant response caused the angel to say, "I am Gabriel. I stand in the presence of God, and I have been sent to speak to you and to tell you this good news. And now you will be silent and not able to speak until the day this happens, because you did not believe my words, which will come true at their appointed time."

Zechariah had been trained to seek God with every fiber of his being, but he struggled to see that the God He sought could make a way where none seemed possible. John the Baptist was about to be born to a once-barren couple.

Believe in the God of the impossible.

SCRIPTURES QUOTED: LUKE 1:7, 19–20

NOT HIDDEN

*For this shall every one that is godly pray unto thee in a time when thou
mayest be found: surely in the floods of great waters they shall not come
nigh unto him. Thou art my hiding place; thou shalt preserve me from
trouble; thou shalt compass me about with songs of deliverance.*

PSALM 32:6–7 KJV

God may not have been hidden from Chip Ingram, but Chip wasn't looking either. His family dynamic kept Jesus in the background. This pastor,
author, and mentor came to faith in Jesus just after high school ended.
As a self-proclaimed workaholic, he became a standout in basketball and
memorized scripture.

God wasn't hidden, but Chip struggled to find Him. He developed hard
rules for himself and embraced the choices of a Pharisee, offending many.
God warned against this kind of self-proclaimed wisdom: "Woe unto them
that are wise in their own eyes, and prudent in their own sight!"

But Chip finally sought God on God's terms. Once Chip understood
that the God of the universe wanted a relationship with him, he began to
grow. God gave him opportunities to help Christians learn what their lives
could look like.

God isn't hidden, and you too can find Him. Seek Him today. It'll become
the best day you experience on earth. "It is good for me to draw near to God:
I have put my trust in the Lord GOD."

SCRIPTURES QUOTED: ISAIAH 5:21; PSALM 73:28

SAVED FROM REBELLION

*Oh, what a miserable person I am! Who will free me from this
life that is dominated by sin and death? Thank God!
The answer is in Jesus Christ our Lord.*

ROMANS 7:24–25 NLT

The best day possible cannot exist in a life dominated by sin. But you have a way out.

Jesus can bring freedom even after you choose to break God's rules. He's given you a path to a better day to come. Without it, the best you can hope for are days filled with guilt and choices defined by rebellion. "There will be very difficult times. For people will love only themselves and their money. They will be boastful and proud, scoffing at God, disobedient to their parents, and ungrateful. They will consider nothing sacred. They will be unloving and unforgiving; they will slander others and have no self-control. They will be cruel and hate what is good. They will betray their friends, be reckless, be puffed up with pride, and love pleasure rather than God. They will act religious, but they will reject the power that could make them godly. Stay away from people like that!"

People may think that money, pride, and cruelty make for their best life, but this is a perfect reminder that God desires a soft heart, humility, and love from His family.

You can get the wrong picture of what makes for your best life. Use today's scripture to help you determine whether your best life here champions the heart of God or your own wish list.

SCRIPTURES QUOTED: 2 TIMOTHY 3:1–5

JAILER RESCUE

The jailer called for lights, rushed in and fell trembling before Paul and Silas. He then brought them out and asked, "Sirs, what must I do to be saved?"

ACTS 16:29–30 NIV

Paul and his missionary partner Silas were thrown in jail for sharing the good news of Jesus. "About midnight Paul and Silas were praying and singing hymns to God, and the other prisoners were listening to them. Suddenly there was such a violent earthquake that the foundations of the prison were shaken. At once all the prison doors flew open, and everyone's chains came loose."

At that time, if a prisoner escaped, the jailer would be killed in his place. The jailer had been sleeping, but the earthquake woke him. When he saw that prisoners could escape, he was ready to take his own life. But Paul shouted, "Don't harm yourself! We are all here!"

Paul and Silas were given a fresh opportunity to share God's salvation—the message that freedom could be found even behind bars. In His wisdom, God positioned two inmates to teach spiritual freedom to a different kind of prisoner.

God sent Jesus to be freedom for the captive, love for the unloved, and kindness for the marginalized. Rescue results in redemption, and salvation brings the surprise of grace. Your best life starts here and never ends, even on the bad days. Remember that whatever chains are binding you—bitterness, unforgiveness, suffering, betrayal—God saves prisoners like you.

SCRIPTURES QUOTED: ACTS 16:25–26, 28

GO

Go ye therefore, and teach all nations, baptizing them in the name of the
Father, and of the Son, and of the Holy Ghost: teaching them to observe
all things whatsoever I have commanded you: and, lo, I am with
you always, even unto the end of the world. Amen.

MATTHEW 28:19–20 KJV

By the world's reckoning, Greg Laurie shouldn't be a preacher. Greg didn't grow up in a Christian home, and his single mother may not have provided the best role model. But he became a Christian, and once on his own, he began to thrive spiritually.

He knew that learning who Jesus is and why He's critical to a friendship with God was paramount. His passion is following the Great Commission. He goes and teaches, trusting the God of the difficult day.

It can be scary to do what God asks, but remember that "the LORD, he it is that doth go before thee; he will be with thee, he will not fail thee, neither forsake thee: fear not, neither be dismayed." When it comes to the salvation God offers, is personal comfort more important than sharing what God can do to a life surrendered to Him? We're not responsible for anyone's decision to follow God, but we are responsible for sharing the transformative power of the Gospel.

How has God changed your life? And who can you share it with?

SCRIPTURE QUOTED: DEUTERONOMY 31:8

GOD IS LOVE

Can anything ever separate us from Christ's love? Does it mean he no longer loves us if we have trouble or calamity, or are persecuted, or hungry, or destitute, or in danger, or threatened with death? . . . No, despite all these things, overwhelming victory is ours through Christ, who loved us.

ROMANS 8:35, 37 NLT

Don't believe the enemy's lie that God only loves you on good days. God's love also reigns victorious in times of trouble, calamity, persecution, hunger, destitution, danger, or death.

If we had only good days and experienced only the things on our gotta-have list, we would never grasp God's love and grace. We wouldn't recognize His awesome power to provide even when we are undeserving of His tender support.

God's mercy is given to the undeserving. His love is offered to all without any need to impress Him with what you can do. He does what you can't, loves when you won't, and forgives when you let go of your bitterness.

"See how very much our Father loves us, for he calls us his children, and that is what we are!" Parents love their children even when they make stupid mistakes. They don't send them away or give up on them. They correct, guide, and redirect. They love their kids because of who they are, not what they've done.

Accept God's love for yourself and then love others. "We love each other because he loved us first."

The best day possible is drenched in the goodness of caring for the people God cares about.

SCRIPTURES QUOTED: 1 JOHN 3:1, 4:19

MUCH FORGIVENESS

*[Jesus said], "Her many sins have been forgiven—as her great love
has shown. But whoever has been forgiven little loves little."*

LUKE 7:47 NIV

You blew it. You'd take back the careless action or hurtful word if you could, but it's too late. The best you can hope for is mercy in the form of forgiveness. You don't deserve it, but if you're not too stubborn, you'll ask for it.

Imagine Jesus stopping by for a meal. In those days, people wore sandals and walked dusty streets cluttered with animal dung. Proper etiquette said that guests were supposed to receive a foot washing. Simon, the host, overlooked this common gesture of hospitality toward Jesus, but he was offended by the humble generosity of a local prostitute. She used her tears and hair to clean Jesus' feet. "If this man were a prophet, he would know who is touching him and what kind of woman she is—that she is a sinner."

Instead of feeling regret for his forgotten hospitality, Simon condemned the woman. . .and thought Jesus should have been more selective in His compassion.

What must Simon's thoughts have been when Jesus looked at the woman and said, "Your faith has saved you; go in peace"?

When we believe we're superior to others, it's easy to think that God doesn't have to forgive us for much. Instead of pride, He desires the offering of a broken and contrite spirit. Out of our humility flows a greater appreciation for Him and His gifts.

SCRIPTURES QUOTED: LUKE 7:39, 50

GOD'S LOVE INSPIRES LOVE

Charity suffereth long, and is kind; charity envieth not; charity
vaunteth not itself, is not puffed up, doth not behave itself unseemly,
seeketh not her own, is not easily provoked, thinketh no evil.

1 CORINTHIANS 13:4–5 KJV

You might think of red kettles and bell ringers when you think of the Salvation Army. But its origins stem from evangelist William Booth, who referred to those who helped him share Jesus as a volunteer army—the Salvation Army.

William often came home from preaching with head wounds after disgruntled people used him for target practice. But in response he created soup kitchens, expressing love in action to those who were just as likely to harm him as listen.

William's best life wasn't avoiding rocks thrown from the crowd. It was knowing that God was working in the streets of London and that the rock throwers were discovering God's love was more impressive than their efforts to silence it.

Jesus said, "Love one another; as I have loved you." William was a follower and love was his banner in 1870s' London. He wanted people to listen to his message because they trusted the action of his love. When people trusted him, they listened and dared to believe God's love was true.

William shared God's love because he knew God: "He that loveth not knoweth not God; for God is love." He knew God, loved Him, and loved people. Follow that example today.

SCRIPTURES QUOTED: JOHN 13:34; 1 JOHN 4:8

ACCEPTED

In this new life, it doesn't matter if you are a Jew or a Gentile,
circumcised or uncircumcised, barbaric, uncivilized, slave,
or free. Christ is all that matters, and he lives in all of us.

COLOSSIANS 3:11 NLT

We're all sinners complete with imperfections and bad days. But God accepts us and calls us His masterpiece. He'll never turn His back on us.

Your ethnic background isn't important to God. Your economic portfolio is never considered, and your personal struggles don't make God wonder if you'll embarrass Him. He accepted you long before you accepted Him. Now He wants you to respond in kind: "Accept each other just as Christ has accepted you so that God will be given glory."

This sense of community contributes to the best day possible when the marginalized aren't left out, the lonely find friendship, and the hurting discover caring conversation. God's acceptance isn't just for your benefit—it's for the benefit of all mankind. It requires you to do what God has done for you.

Want to make your day even better? Jesus said, "Those the Father has given me will come to me, and I will never reject them." You will never feel the sting of rejection from Jesus.

If you don't believe that, you might just be thinking God's Word isn't true. But God can't lie, and He said He *never* rejects family. He accepts sinners, and He won't leave you without help in your new life with Him.

SCRIPTURES QUOTED: ROMANS 15:7; JOHN 6:37

YOU NEEDED ACCEPTANCE

While Jesus was having dinner at Levi's house, many tax collectors
and sinners were eating with him and his disciples,
for there were many who followed him.

MARK 2:15 NIV

The religious leaders couldn't believe the scandal Jesus was causing. He'd decided to eat a meal in the home of His most recent follower, a tax collector named Levi. "Why does he eat with tax collectors and sinners?" they asked.

Probably because tax collectors and sinners needed rescue just as much as the questioning religious leaders. Jesus told them, "It is not the healthy who need a doctor, but the sick. I have not come to call the righteous, but sinners."

Jesus said that everyone needed rescue. And the religious leaders heard that Jesus came for the worst people on the planet. Jesus championed the needy—and the religious leaders didn't think their God would behave like that. But He *did*.

This former tax collector became one of Jesus' disciples. You may know this man as Matthew. Some scholars believe he was used by God to write the first book in the New Testament.

The key takeaway of this story is that Jesus accepted society's unacceptable. He hung out with them because they needed Him. He loved them because many of them needed to experience love.

Your best life possible is knowing that God sent His Son to accept people and allow them to accept Him. He came to rescue the perishing. He came because you needed Him.

SCRIPTURES QUOTED: MARK 2:16, 17

ACCEPTANCE THERAPY

If we walk in the light, as he is in the light, we have fellowship one with another, and the blood of Jesus Christ his Son cleanseth us from all sin.

1 JOHN 1:7 KJV

James was the son of a strict preacher and had no desire to follow in his father's footsteps. He wanted to find acceptance as a lawyer. He was on his way to making this a reality when his father passed away. He felt responsible for taking care of his family.

His best prospects seemed to be working as a store clerk. Eventually, he owned a shop of his own then a small company with stores in three locations. Under his leadership, the stores grew from three to more than thirty. He later surpassed one thousand stores before the Great Depression smashed the American economy in 1929.

James struggled to gain acceptance from his father. And he thought he'd found acceptance in business, but the crash sent him to the hospital a broken man. He borrowed money to pay his employees, but in the case of James Cash Penney, the synthesis of many events finally led him to accept God's love while recuperating in the hospital. His faith sustained him during difficult days, but it's God's acceptance that means the most to those who feel like outsiders. "The people that walked in darkness have seen a great light: they that dwell in the land of the shadow of death, upon them hath the light shined." Jesus is the light, and He accepts all who are drawn to His light.

SCRIPTURE QUOTED: ISAIAH 9:2

PROTECTED

Those who live in the shelter of the Most High will find rest in the shadow of the Almighty. . . . He will cover you with his feathers. He will shelter you with his wings. His faithful promises are your armor and protection.

PSALM 91:1, 4 NLT

As followers of Jesus, we rest in the Father's protection. Don't be debilitated by the belief that you're alone and vulnerable to attack. Although fear is natural when our understanding is limited, you can trust the One who knows the outcome of every decision you'll ever make.

When you understand that God knows everything—and therefore isn't afraid of anything—you'll also know that nothing takes Him by surprise. Nothing could ever defeat Him. Can you see the foolishness in thinking your greatest challenges are too difficult for God? Jesus said, "Life is more than food, and your body more than clothing. Look at the ravens. They don't plant or harvest or store food in barns, for God feeds them. And you are far more valuable to him than any birds!"

God protects birds and makes sure they are fed. Don't you think He could protect you? Live in His shelter as you rest in His shadow. Take up His armor and be protected.

We've all been hurt at some point, so don't think God's protection turns you into a superhero. His protection is love that cares more deeply for you than anyone can, encourages more than anyone else will, and withstands the worst that His adversary can come up with.

SCRIPTURES QUOTED: LUKE 12:23–24

THE PROTECTION PROMISE

*By faith the prostitute Rahab, because she welcomed the spies,
was not killed with those who were disobedient.*

HEBREWS 11:31 NIV

Rahab was a sinner. And she wasn't part of God's family. But by faith she was welcomed not only into His family but into the line of Jesus Christ.

Joshua sent spies to Jericho to provide intel on a city that God promised would be theirs. The local king had his own intel and knew there were spies in town. It was just a matter of time before they were located and punished. Chances were strong they wouldn't survive. But the duo encountered someone willing to hide them. Rahab believed God had given the land to these foreigners. She suspected the entire city would be destroyed. So she asked, "Please swear to me by the LORD that you will show kindness to my family, because I have shown kindness to you."

She requested protection and hope for a future for herself and her family. The spies promised, "If you don't tell what we are doing, we will treat you kindly and faithfully when the LORD gives us the land."

Then Joshua and the Israelites quietly marched around the city as the people of Jericho watched. God had given specific instructions for their march. On the last day, horns bellowed just before the crumbling of the city walls. The promise of protection was honored, and Rahab and her family were safely taken from the city before its destruction. God can protect.

SCRIPTURES QUOTED: JOSHUA 2:12, 14

GOD HELPS THOSE WHO ASK

The angel of the LORD encampeth round about them that fear him,
and delivereth them. O taste and see that the LORD is
good: blessed is the man that trusteth in him.

PSALM 34:7–8 KJV

Have you ever had hard questions and couldn't find the answers? God may have some things to teach you first. George Washington Carver was a scientist and a Christian. He often asked questions but once acknowledged, "Years ago I went into my laboratory and said, 'Dear Mr. Creator, please tell me what the universe was made for?' The Great Creator answered, 'You want to know too much for that little mind of yours. Ask for something more your size, little man.'"

His ways are higher than our ways, and His infinite knowledge and precise planning can't be grasped by our limited human minds. We see pain, loss, and suffering and wonder what purpose it serves. But maybe it's enough to know that God does protect, has protected, and will continue to protect. "The LORD. . .shall preserve thy soul. The LORD shall preserve thy going out and thy coming in from this time forth, and even for evermore." Sadly, we sometimes step outside of His protection when we try to manage things without His help.

Know this—God can protect you from a bad job, an accident, fear, lies, and the attack of the enemy. But it's also important to remember that some things you face are meant to hone your endurance. When you need God's protection, ask—He will never leave you or forsake you.

George Washington Carver was protected when people criticized him for being a scientist who also believed in God. History remembers him for both.

SCRIPTURES QUOTED: PSALM 121:7–8

ASSURED

His Spirit joins with our spirit to affirm that we are God's children. And since
we are his children, we are his heirs. In fact, together with Christ we are heirs
of God's glory. But if we are to share his glory, we must also share his suffering.
ROMANS 8:16—17 NLT

God has experienced pain. He suffered the broken relationship with the first humans when they thought they knew more than He did. He watched His Son die because humanity broke His law.

Jesus was the link between a good God and broken people. This same God became a Father to someone like you. You're His heir, and your inheritance awaits you in heaven. But God's Word is clear—you'll also share His suffering. You'll have seasons of disappointment. You may even suffer the loss of a relationship because of sin. You've suffered because you once kept your distance from His Son.

God never wanted distance from you. God's Spirit can assure yours that there's something greater than simply the idea of God—this is a God who's trustworthy, kind, and forgiving.

This is a perfect final assurance: "Even before he made the world, God loved us and chose us in Christ to be holy and without fault in his eyes. God decided in advance to adopt us into his own family by bringing us to himself through Jesus Christ. This is what he wanted to do, and it gave him great pleasure."

SCRIPTURES QUOTED: EPHESIANS 1:4—5

CONVINCED FOR A LIFETIME

*I, John, your brother and companion in the suffering and kingdom
and patient endurance that are ours in Jesus, was on the island of
Patmos because of the word of God and the testimony of Jesus.*

REVELATION 1:9 NIV

Jesus and John had been the best of friends. And John had served his Friend well. He penned the Gospel of John, as well as First, Second, and Third John. After all the other disciples moved on to their better day, John lived as a prisoner on the island of Patmos. There, he had another assignment—to write the book of Revelation. God revealed to John amazing things that he struggled to explain.

John was faithful to Jesus' teachings. There's no evidence he ever denied God. When John began to follow the Lord, he was convinced that Jesus had life-giving words that he later recorded, words like, "I am the light of the world. Whoever follows me will never walk in darkness, but will have the light of life." John didn't need to walk in darkness because he followed in the footsteps of his Creator.

It seems like it would've been easy for John to turn his back on someone he knew for only a few years when he was younger. But John remained faithful. Why? Because "the Son of God has come and has given us understanding, so that we may know him who is true. And we are in him who is true by being in his Son Jesus Christ. He is the true God and eternal life."

SCRIPTURES QUOTED: JOHN 8:12; 1 JOHN 5:20

ASSURED TO THE END

Two are better than one; because they have a good reward for their labour.
For if they fall, the one will lift up his fellow: but woe to him that is
alone when he falleth; for he hath not another to help him up. . . .
And if one prevail against him, two shall withstand him;
and a threefold cord is not quickly broken.

ECCLESIASTES 4:9–10, 12 KJV

James Chuma and Abdullah Susi were faithful to missionary David Livingstone. They followed him across the continent of Africa. And they were with him when he died in 1873.

These two Africans had to be assured that David was worth following just as David was assured that God was worth following. David freed James from slavery as a child and became the young boy's only family. James stayed with the missionary until he died. Abdulla had been hired to help David, and he too stayed with the missionary, ultimately helping to carry his body back to the coast so it could be returned to England.

Perhaps Chuma and Susi had heard David's prayer: "God, send me anywhere, only go with me. Lay any burden on me, only sustain me. And sever any tie in my heart except the tie that binds my heart to Yours."

The missionary loved Chuma and Susi like family as his health declined. Perhaps he remembered what God said: "Above all things have fervent charity among yourselves: for charity shall cover the multitude of sins. Use hospitality one to another without grudging. As every man hath received the gift, even so minister the same one to another."

SCRIPTURES QUOTED: 1 PETER 4:8–10

GOD SPEAKS

Fear God and obey his commands, for this is everyone's duty.
ECCLESIASTES 12:13 NLT

Do you ever wonder if God speaks? Abraham and Moses heard God's voice, so we know that He does speak. But for most this just doesn't happen. And sometimes when we have a problem, God seems silent. We wonder why we should even ask God for help if He leaves us to guess.

But God doesn't abandon us. He said following is our duty, and He's clear about what His rules are. Consider the words of Jesus: "My sheep listen to my voice; I know them, and they follow me." Follow the God you hear—and if you can't hear Him then keep listening.

Just as parents can pick out the voice of their child in a crowded room, you can also tune your ear to the voice of your heavenly Father. God speaks to us through scripture, His living Word: "I send it out, and it always produces fruit. It will accomplish all I want it to, and it will prosper everywhere I send it." What God needed to say He said in the Bible. That means when you want to know what He thinks, you should pray and ask for help. Then open a Bible or click a scripture app and read His words about what concerns you.

God speaks. He has answers. And you don't need to look for signs and wonders. Read the Bible. The best life possible improves by knowing what God says and what He wants. And always remember that the best you could ever experience here has an expiration date. A better day *is* coming.

SCRIPTURES QUOTED: JOHN 10:27; ISAIAH 55:11

LATE-NIGHT LISTENING

The LORD came and stood there, calling as at the other times, "Samuel! Samuel!" Then Samuel said, "Speak, for your servant is listening."

1 SAMUEL 3:10 NIV

Young Samuel helped the priest, Eli. One night as he slept, he heard someone call his name. Samuel thought it was the priest, but after Samuel interrupted the old man's sleep, Eli was convinced *God* was speaking. Eli said, "Go and lie down, and if he calls you, say, 'Speak, LORD, for your servant is listening.'"

Samuel learned to recognize God's voice, and when he became a man, he delivered God's words as His prophet. God says, "If you accept my words and store up my commands within you, turning your ear to wisdom and applying your heart to understanding—indeed, if you call out for insight and cry aloud for understanding, and if you look for it as for silver and search for it as for hidden treasure, then you will understand the fear of the LORD and find the knowledge of God."

Hearing God isn't a passive action. Get involved—pray, read, and learn.

The words you've read will return to your mind and seep into your soul. His words will speak to your need—at just the right time. This is not a magic formula. Rather it's the primary way God speaks.

Maybe you think you don't need the help. You can relegate your Bible to the role of a perpetual dust collector. But God has wisdom for every step you take, so pick up His Word, shake off the dust, and discover His plans for you.

SCRIPTURES QUOTED: 1 SAMUEL 3:9; PROVERBS 2:1–5

THE DOWNCAST CONFLICT

Bear ye one another's burdens, and so fulfil the law of Christ.
GALATIANS 6:2 KJV

If you could have your best life now, you'd be happy, right? After all, good circumstances bring a smile. But what would your comfort mean to someone who's not experiencing that same best-life scenario? Physician and playwright Anton Chekhov thought that "at the door of every happy person there should be a man with a hammer whose knock would serve as a constant reminder of the existence of unfortunate people."

God also cares for the downcast: "He healeth the broken in heart, and bindeth up their wounds." Rejoice when someone rejoices. Be sensitive enough to mourn when others are suffering loss. Not everyone will be happy at the same time. Not everyone will feel broken together or get good news at the same time. Don't let joy and mourning become competitors.

Jesus said, "Blessed are the poor in spirit: for theirs is the kingdom of heaven. Blessed are they that mourn: for they shall be comforted." Author C. S. Lewis wrote about his grief after the loss of his wife, Joy: "Part of every misery is, so to speak, the misery's shadow or reflection: the fact that you don't merely suffer but have to keep on thinking about the fact that you suffer. I not only live each endless day in grief, but live each day thinking about living each day in grief."

Love others by being sensitive to their emotions—both their trials and triumphs. Support them in their laughter and tears.

SCRIPTURES QUOTED: PSALM 147:3; MATTHEW 5:3–4

For I cried out to him for help, praising him as I spoke. If I had not confessed
the sin in my heart, the Lord would not have listened. But God did listen!
He paid attention to my prayer. Praise God, who did not ignore
my prayer or withdraw his unfailing love from me.

PSALM 66:17–20 NLT

Confessing sin could be as simple as admitting God was right and you were wrong. We recognize our offense and decide not to continue doing it. The real point to confession is that no matter how many times you blow it, you keep coming back to God—because He will always listen. He always has time for us.

He pays attention to the details of our lives and doesn't ignore our prayers. And He won't take back His love. God said, "If you look for me wholeheartedly, you will find me." He also said, "I am with you always, even to the end of the age."

God can be found, and He sticks with you when others walk away. If you think prayer isn't effective, consider what William Temple wrote: "When I pray, coincidences happen, and when I don't, they don't."

God doesn't orchestrate coincidence—He directs circumstances. But at times we act as if the best things in life aren't hand-delivered by God. Are you more likely to thank your lucky stars before you thank God? Include regular conversation with God into your day so He can hear you. (And then read your Bible so you can hear Him.)

SCRIPTURES QUOTED: JEREMIAH 29:13; MATTHEW 28:20

GOD LISTENS

"If my people, who are called by my name, will humble themselves and pray and seek my face and turn from their wicked ways, then I will hear from heaven, and I will forgive their sin and will heal their land."

2 CHRONICLES 7:14 NIV

Israel was stumbling in a time of national sin, and lawbreaking was spreading with the force of an epidemic. No one seemed interested in curing their rebellion through repentance. But the promise of hope arrived in God's words: "I will hear from heaven, and I will forgive."

Prayer isn't only a personal conversation with God. Sometimes we pray corporately with others. As the body of Christ we are to "confess [our] sins to each other and pray for each other so that you may be healed. The prayer of a righteous person is powerful and effective."

Did you notice the word *healed*? It carries the idea of restoration, fixing what's broken, or making new. Talk to God in your state of brokenness: "In my distress I called to the LORD; I cried to my God for help. From his temple he heard my voice; my cry came before him, into his ears."

The Israelites didn't want to turn from their wickedness. They didn't want to agree that God was right and they were wrong. But God says, "If anyone turns a deaf ear to my instruction, even their prayers are detestable." Ask God to reveal to you the hidden sins of your heart.

SCRIPTURES QUOTED: JAMES 5:16; PSALM 18:6; PROVERBS 28:9

GOD OF THE SMALL THINGS

Hear me when I call, O God of my righteousness: thou hast enlarged me when I was in distress; have mercy upon me, and hear my prayer.

PSALM 4:1 KJV

Daniel Webster Whittle once wrote, "The mistake of Christians is in not praying over little things. Consult God about everything. Expect His counsel, His guidance, His care, His provision, His deliverance, His blessing, in everything."

Daniel was an author and evangelist, and his hymns are still sung today.

Major Whittle, as he was known during the Civil War, was invited to the bedside of a dying soldier to pray. But at the time, Daniel wasn't a Christian. He cautiously began to pray, and by the end of the prayer, Daniel had a relationship with Jesus. It seemed God used a dying soldier to bring Daniel to the foot of the cross, where he found new life. It's what God wanted.

Daniel became friends with D. L. Moody, and he prayed, knowing he should "ask in faith, nothing wavering. For he that wavereth is like a wave of the sea driven with the wind and tossed." Without faith, we are out of control with no real destination.

Daniel Whittle was a man of prayer who experienced a connection to God through music. He identified with this wisdom from the apostle Paul: "I will pray with the spirit, and I will pray with the understanding also: I will sing with the spirit, and I will sing with the understanding also." Pray and sing praise in response to God's unrivaled goodness.

Scriptures quoted: James 1:6; 1 Corinthians 14:15

THE BLESSING

"May the LORD bless you and protect you. May the LORD smile on you and be gracious to you. May the LORD show you his favor and give you his peace."

NUMBERS 6:24—26 NLT

Your best life possible includes blessings—both received and given. "All praise to God, the Father of our Lord Jesus Christ, who has blessed us with every spiritual blessing in the heavenly realms because we are united with Christ." Blessings are not *one-way* gifts. You've been blessed—bless someone else.

If you believe God could ever run out of blessings, consider something A. W. Tozer wrote: "An infinite God can give all of Himself to each of His children. He does not distribute Himself that each may have a part, but to each one He gives all of Himself as fully as if there were no others." No one is left out.

How exactly do you bless others? "When God's people are in need, be ready to help them. Always be eager to practice hospitality." This isn't the only way to bless those around you, but it's a great place to start.

When you seek only your own blessing from God—when you refuse to bless others by lending a hand when they need it—your showers of blessing may dry up. In generosity, hold open your hands. Allow God's blessing to flow through them to others.

SCRIPTURES QUOTED: EPHESIANS 1:3; ROMANS 12:13

GENERATIONAL BLESSING

By faith Enoch was taken from this life, so that he did not experience death:
"He could not be found, because God had taken him away." For before he
was taken, he was commended as one who pleased God.

HEBREWS 11:5 NIV

Enoch was the great-grandfather of Moses. God's Word says that Enoch pleased God and describes him as a man of faith.

There are only two men who exited their time on earth without passing through death's door. Elijah was taken in a chariot of fire, and "Enoch walked faithfully with God; then he was no more, because God took him away."

Enoch was blessed because he was a blessing. He modeled faithfulness to his son Methuselah, who then modeled it for his son Lamech, who modeled it for his son Noah, who "found favor in the eyes of the LORD."

Blessings and curses are both generational. One speaks life and the other, death. Maybe you've never had life-enhancing blessings spoken by parents or family, but God can step in where they may have checked out. He's a "father to the fatherless, a defender of widows."

You can learn how to live God's best for you by allowing God to be your father. His teaching will become a generational blessing to your family. Allow Him to reshape the way you speak life into your family. And His transformation of your life and the lives of your family members is truly a blessing beyond compare.

SCRIPTURES QUOTED: GENESIS 5:24, 6:8; PSALM 68:5

SHOVELS AND CARTS

The mercy of the LORD is from everlasting to everlasting upon them that fear him, and his righteousness unto children's children.

PSALM 103:17 KJV

It has been said that you can never out-give God. And you may have heard that God can do more with a tithe than you can with what's left. There's power in His blessing.

Charles Spurgeon wrote, "God has a way of giving by the cartloads to those who give away by shovelfuls." What you give may be received with great appreciation, and the gifts you receive are worthy of your personal gratitude. But sometimes the obvious response doesn't happen, and a link in a blessing chain gets broken.

Spurgeon was a young man when he started preaching. The congregation at New Park Street Chapel asked him to preach and then extended a welcome for him to preach six more months. They kept extending his time at the church until his death at the age of fifty-seven. The church was blessed with growth as the congregation grew from 232 to more than 5,000 under Spurgeon's leadership.

The blessings weren't founded on numbers but by the people who grew to love God and serve others. Spurgeon used the example of George Müller and started an orphanage that blessed many children until it was destroyed in World War II.

Charles Spurgeon sought to bless because God had been a blessing. The Lord's words from the book of Jeremiah probably meant a lot to him: "I have loved thee with an everlasting love: therefore with lovingkindness have I drawn thee." Those words might just mean something to you too.

SCRIPTURES QUOTED: JEREMIAH 31:3

THE INHERITANCE

*Because we are united with Christ, we have received an inheritance
from God, for he chose us in advance, and he makes
everything work out according to his plan.*

EPHESIANS 1:11 NLT

Do you believe that Jesus is God's Son, that He came to earth, was sacrificed for every law broken by man, and then defeated death? What you believe is important. An inheritance comes to an heir usually when someone dies. In their death, Christians may pass on an inheritance to their family. But what they give up on earth is a very small thing compared to what they gain from God's inheritance on that better day to come.

But you inherit some of God's blessings here too. "[Thank] the Father. He has enabled you to share in the inheritance that belongs to his people, who live in the light." You reflect His character, observe His miracles, and experience His peace. William Barclay brought sense to the concept when he wrote, "For the Christian, heaven is where Jesus is. We do not need to speculate on what heaven will be like. It is enough to know that we will be forever with Him."

How is it possible to be forever with Jesus? "He generously poured out the Spirit upon us through Jesus Christ our Savior. Because of his grace he made us right in his sight and gave us confidence that we will inherit eternal life." Christians are forgiven, have eternal life, and experience God's love. God's inheritance for Christians is a promise.

SCRIPTURES QUOTED: COLOSSIANS 1:12; TITUS 3:6—7

SARAH'S STORY

By faith even Sarah, who was past childbearing age, was enabled to bear children because she considered him faithful who had made the promise.
HEBREWS 11:11 NIV

God made Sarah's husband, Abraham, a promise: "I will make you into a great nation, and. . .you will be a blessing." But Sarah was growing old and had no children. She wondered where this great nation would come from.

The couple tried alternatives that were outside of God's plan to "help" Him keep His promise. When Sarah was planning her ninetieth birthday party, God delivered a message to Abraham: "I will surely return to you about this time next year, and Sarah your wife will have a son."

Sarah laughed. Was it disbelief? Did the idea seem so unlikely that it jolted her funny bone? Was it nervous laughter followed by tears? Whatever it was, the hall of faith names Sarah as one who "considered him faithful who had made the promise."

Her only son, Isaac, whose name means "laughter," was this promised inheritance that led to a great nation—a fulfilled promise through which others were blessed.

Sarah and Abraham had plenty of struggles, tears, and stretching of their faith. So take heart on those days when you wonder if following God has been worth it. Remember that when Sarah could have easily been convinced to give up, God showed up with a birth announcement. Hang on.

SCRIPTURES QUOTED: GENESIS 12:2, 18:10; HEBREWS 11:11

THE LOSS AND THE GAIN

The LORD is the portion of mine inheritance and
of my cup: thou maintainest my lot.

PSALM 16:5 KJV

William Borden was raised in wealth. His dad made millions mining silver in Colorado. William's mother also had great wealth of a different kind. She discovered her lifelong faith when William was a child, and her influence invited William to follow.

A trip around the world when William was sixteen awakened in him a passion for world missions. This dedication was visible to those who knew him. Charles Erdman was a professor at Princeton who wrote of William, "His judgment was so unerring and so mature that I always forgot there was such a difference in our ages. His complete consecration and devotion to Christ were a revelation to me, and his confidence in prayer a continual inspiration."

William was headed toward a missionary role in China. This dream faded in Egypt, where he contracted cerebral meningitis in 1913.

Some say that William wrote three phrases in his Bible: "*No reserve*" to express his commitment to missions, "*No retreat*" to show his willingness to lose his family inheritance, and "*No regrets*" to follow God even if it meant death.

Jesus had His own thoughts on this kind of sacrifice: "Every one that hath forsaken houses, or brethren, or sisters, or father, or mother, or wife, or children, or lands, for my name's sake, shall receive an hundredfold, and shall inherit everlasting life."

William Borden's life proved the truth that the inheritance waiting for him was greater than anything he could lose on earth.

SCRIPTURE QUOTED: MATTHEW 19:29

THE STRENGTH OF ENCOURAGEMENT

For I can do everything through Christ, who gives me strength.
Even so, you have done well to share with me in my present difficulty.
PHILIPPIANS 4:13–14 NLT

You've probably read Philippians 4:13 and concluded that you and God can tackle anything together. You're not wrong, but the second verse is largely overlooked and may be one of the ways God uses to give you strength.

Family and friends can play a key role in helping you through life. God can use them to encourage you on the hard days. God gives you strength and then invites others to walk with you during dark nights, stormy days, and when you need a reminder that there's a better day coming. "Let us think of ways to motivate one another to acts of love and good works."

Encouragement is more than a motivational poster or a social media post. It means working through tough issues, developing a better perspective, and refusing to disengage when a hurting friend pushes you away. "May God, who gives this patience and encouragement, help you live in complete harmony with each other, as is fitting for followers of Christ Jesus."

There really is something to the idea of "paying it forward" with acts of kindness. Albert Schweitzer wrote: "Whoever is spared personal pain must feel himself called to help in diminishing the pain of others. We must all carry our share of the misery which lies upon the world."

SCRIPTURE QUOTED: HEBREWS 10:24; ROMANS 15:5

BEGIN WITH HIS STRENGTH

The Samaritan woman said to him, "You are a Jew and I am
a Samaritan woman. How can you ask me for a drink?"
(For Jews do not associate with Samaritans.)
JOHN 4:9 NIV

Jesus took His disciples outside their comfort zone in Samaria. He sat by Jacob's well while the disciples went to get food. The Samaritans had roots going back into Jewish history, but they differed in the expression and location of their worship. If you were a Jew, you had nothing to do with a Samaritan. And Samaritans were used to the rejection.

Yet when the Samaritan woman came to Jacob's well, she heard Jesus say, "Will you give me a drink?" She was a sinner, a Samaritan, and had different views on worship. She didn't understand why a Jewish man would talk to her.

Jesus didn't reject her. Instead He invited her into greater conversation: "Everyone who drinks this water will be thirsty again, but whoever drinks the water I give them will never thirst. Indeed, the water I give them will become in them a spring of water welling up to eternal life."

Naturally she was curious about "living water." She wanted what He offered and brought friends to learn more from the One who knew everything about her.

When the woman asked if He was the Messiah, Jesus declared, "I, the one speaking to you—I am he." Her best day possible began with *His* knowledge and strength.

SCRIPTURE QUOTED: JOHN 4:7, 13–14, 26

STRENGTH IN GRACE

Grow in grace, and in the knowledge of our Lord and Saviour
Jesus Christ. To him be glory both now and for ever. Amen.

2 PETER 3:18 KJV

Many who meet Max Lucado feel as if they're meeting an old friend. His gentleness and kindness are evident. Max took a strong grip on grace and discovered more. "Be strong in the grace that is in Christ Jesus. And the things that thou hast heard of me among many witnesses, the same commit thou to faithful men, who shall be able to teach others also. Thou therefore endure hardness, as a good soldier of Jesus Christ."

Max wanted to become a missionary. After he met and married his wife, Denalyn, the two set off to minister in Brazil. It seemed he was doing exactly what he was supposed to do, but God had other plans.

Word arrived that Max's dad had passed away, so Max and his family moved home to support his mom. He took up a new ministry as a pastor.

Max has been described as "America's pastor." But a heart as grace-oriented as his first had to marinate in personal pain while identifying with the sorrow others experience. He chooses to speak words of hope when suffering tries to diminish the light of God's love. Max could easily say with Peter, "Grace and peace be multiplied unto you through the knowledge of God, and of Jesus our Lord."

God's grace grants access to a strength you'll need when despair finds you.

SCRIPTURES QUOTED: 2 TIMOTHY 2:1–3; 2 PETER 1:2

PERSONAL ATTENTION

The Lord directs the steps of the godly. He delights in every detail of their lives.
Though they stumble, they will never fall, for the Lord holds them by the hand.

PSALM 37:23–24 NLT

Arriving at a new destination requires either a map or a guide. And believers have the reassurance that not only does God know the way, He's holding our hand for every step.

Just as a father folds his child's small fingers protectively in his palm and guides him along, our heavenly Father directs our steps. His wisdom surpasses ours, and we can rest easily under His guidance. He loves to lavish us with His attention. "You, O Lord, are a God of compassion and mercy, slow to get angry and filled with unfailing love and faithfulness." God Himself holds your hand. "For I hold you by your right hand—I, the Lord your God. And I say to you, 'Don't be afraid. I am here to help you.'"

If all this personal attention seems impossible to believe, God also gives you direct access to His Spirit, who is our counselor, guide, helper, and teacher.

What benefit would there be in following God if He didn't have answers, if He didn't know the directions, or if there was no hope of getting to your better day to come? If God doesn't have answers, then why has the Christian faith continued to change lives, meet needs, and strengthen families? Know this: God has the answers you're looking for.

SCRIPTURES QUOTED: PSALM 86:15; ISAIAH 41:13

CAN'T MISS IT

When the angels had left them and gone into heaven, the shepherds said
to one another, "Let's go to Bethlehem and see this thing that
has happened, which the Lord has told us about."

LUKE 2:15 NIV

Shepherds were social outcasts. They were considered perpetually unclean because of their work with animals, and then there was the smell. They didn't make it to town often and spent their nights with the sheep.

But when an angel announced the birth of the Messiah, the joyous news was shared first with these lowly sheep herders. "Do not be afraid. I bring you good news that will cause great joy for all the people. Today in the town of David a Savior has been born to you; he is the Messiah, the Lord."

With no time to prepare, make a gift, or even bathe in a stream, the shepherds followed the brightest star in the night sky to a place just outside a local inn. They found a couple, a baby, and a makeshift crib. This was God's Son. God's messenger angels celebrated, "Glory to God in the highest heaven, and on earth peace to those on whom his favor rests."

You've probably heard this story at least once a year for most of your life. But don't let familiarity dull the power of its truth. God loves everyone, no matter their background. And He has life-altering directions for everyone.

SCRIPTURES QUOTED: LUKE 2:10–11, 14

CONTENT OR COMPLACENT

Thus saith the LORD, thy Redeemer, the Holy One of Israel; I am the LORD thy God which teacheth thee to profit, which leadeth thee by the way that thou shouldest go.

ISAIAH 48:17 KJV

Each of us possesses skills that God can use. After all, He gave them to us. Honoring Him with your time, talent, and resources seems appropriate. "Thou shalt love the Lord thy God with all thy heart, and with all thy soul, and with all thy mind, and with all thy strength: this is the first commandment."

Keith and Kristyn Getty were born and raised in Ireland. It was a culture they were familiar with among people they actually knew. Yet God's plan was to take them beyond the borders of Ireland to share something some people weren't even sure was needed—modern hymns.

Loving God will often mean changing your personal direction. It will mean going where He's going. God desires that we learn *contentment*, but we often confuse that with *complacency*. Contentment is being satisfied where God places you. But complacency means you have no intention of doing anything more than you're doing right now. But if this life is God's big adventure for you, you can't climb spiritual mountains while watching from the lodge window.

It's estimated that, in churches each year, more than fifty million people sing songs that the Gettys wrote. If this couple did what most were doing, they wouldn't have written hymns. If they had done what was comfortable, they'd have stayed in Ireland.

Instead they followed God.

SCRIPTURE QUOTED: MARK 12:30

The Holy Spirit produces this kind of fruit in our lives: love, joy,
peace, patience, kindness, goodness, faithfulness, gentleness,
and self-control. There is no law against these things!

GALATIANS 5:22—23 NLT

It doesn't help to believe that God has a plan and can direct you if you have no intention of following Him. Your best day possible includes moving in God's direction—not trying to convince Him that He should stamp His approval on your plans. God doesn't answer to you. But He is inviting you to something better than this moment.

The Holy Spirit provides the guidance, or fruit, you need to follow God. This isn't a pick-your-favorite-flavor deal. Those who walk with Jesus can exhibit *all* of His characteristics: love, joy, peace, patience, kindness, goodness, faithfulness, gentleness, and self-control. These traits are so universally appealing, no law has been written to ban them.

Jesus promised, "I will ask the Father, and he will give you another Advocate, who will never leave you. He is the Holy Spirit, who leads into all truth. The world cannot receive him, because it isn't looking for him and doesn't recognize him. But you know him."

God has given you everything you need to experience His abundant life as you wait for the better day to come. Develop the fruit of God's Spirit. Let others observe and judge: "Just as you can identify a tree by its fruit, so you can identify people by their actions."

SCRIPTURES QUOTED: JOHN 14:16—17; MATTHEW 7:20

BITTER FRUIT RECLAIMED

*The two women went on until they came to Bethlehem. When they arrived
in Bethlehem, the whole town was stirred because of them,
and the women exclaimed, "Can this be Naomi?"*

RUTH 1:19 NIV

Naomi's life had grown bitter. Her sons were dead and she was a widow
in a foreign land. Even when her widowed daughter-in-law Ruth said she
wanted to go with her, Naomi wasn't convinced. Naomi followed God to
Bethlehem simply because it seemed practical.

She wouldn't claim the best day possible. In fact, she had an unusual
request: "Don't call me Naomi [which means "pleasant"]. Call me Mara
[which means "bitter"], because the Almighty has made my life very bitter."

When Naomi decided to help Ruth, the older woman's hope was re-
kindled. Life began to return to the broken widow. When Naomi stopped
feeding bitterness, she found she could praise and participate in life again.

God never promised a pain-free life. Pain finds us all in the course of
time. But God is trustworthy and strong. He can take any circumstance and
reshape it into something good—even when you messed up.

God redeemed Naomi's bitter fruit. After her daughter-in-law Ruth
remarried, God ultimately gave Naomi a grandson, Obed: "Then Naomi
took the child in her arms and cared for him."

If you are skeptical that God has a better day to come, you aren't the
first. But God has a plan that can move you from bitter to better. Ask Him
to show you the way.

SCRIPTURES QUOTED: RUTH 1:20, 4:16

ONE LIFE

Be strong and of a good courage, fear not, nor be afraid of them: for the Lord thy God, he it is that doth go with thee; he will not fail thee, nor forsake thee.

DEUTERONOMY 31:6 KJV

"Only one life, 'twill soon be past, only what's done for Christ will last. And when I am dying, how happy I'll be, if the lamp of my life has been burned out for Thee."

That's the joy of finishing well. There's just one life, and one day it will end. And you can take with you only the things that bear God's fingerprints. When your last breath is exhaled, there will be joy knowing you walked with God.

The author of that poem was missionary C. T. Studd. He was a risk taker, a bold proclaimer, and God's soldier. His life echoed the psalm, "My soul followeth hard after thee: thy right hand upholdeth me."

C. T. followed and God provided. He believed God was trustworthy. "Blessed is the man that walketh not in the counsel of the ungodly, nor standeth in the way of sinners, nor sitteth in the seat of the scornful. But his delight is in the law of the Lord; and in his law doth he meditate day and night."

C. T. Studd demonstrated that he was totally at peace with God's ability to provide throughout this life, until that day when he would meet his Savior face-to-face.

SCRIPTURES QUOTED: PSALM 63:8, 1:1—2

THE END ZONE

Since God chose you to be the holy people he loves, you must clothe yourselves
with tenderhearted mercy, kindness, humility, gentleness, and patience.
Make allowance for each other's faults, and forgive anyone who offends you.
Remember, the Lord forgave you, so you must forgive others. Above all,
clothe yourselves with love, which binds us all together in perfect harmony.
And let the peace that comes from Christ rule in your hearts.

COLOSSIANS 3:12–15 NLT

Sometimes we're frustrated by others, and just as often we're the culprit of
another's frustration. We need to both give and receive forgiveness. Just
make sure your wardrobe doesn't need adjusted.

God's Word says to clothe yourself in mercy, kindness, humbleness,
gentleness, and patience. Forgiveness looks good on you, and love brings
people together.

God is good, His plan is perfect, and His love is great. His grace is amazing,
and His mercies are an everyday miracle. If the theme of this book could
be contained in one sentence, it might well be these words from Albert
Barnes: "Life, if properly viewed in any aspect, is great, but mainly great
when viewed in its relation to the world to come."

Follow God's plan to a better future. It's a promise—a guarantee. It in-
stills hope and demands endurance. It perseveres and is grounded in trust.

This has been an affirming journey, and you've followed through to the
end. When you long for the better day to come, pray to God, who "will keep
in perfect peace all who trust in you, all whose thoughts are fixed on you!
Trust in the LORD always."

SCRIPTURES QUOTED: ISAIAH 26:3–4

SCRIPTURE INDEX

Proverbs

ABOUT THE AUTHOR

Glenn A. Hascall is an accomplished writer with credits in more than 130 books. He is a broadcast veteran and voice actor and is actively involved in audio drama.

HELP FOR HARD TIMES

Here's a practical guide of short prayer starters that will help men pray confidently during difficult times. From illness and relationship issues to struggles with self-worth and daily life stresses, dozens of topics are covered. Each section opens with a short devotional thought and applicable scripture.

Paperback / 978-1-64352-510-5 / $5.99